First World War
and Army of Occupation
War Diary
France, Belgium and Germany

23 DIVISION
Divisional Troops
101 Field Company Royal Engineers
25 August 1915 - 31 October 1917

WO95/2177/1

The Naval & Military Press Ltd
www.nmarchive.com
Published in association with The National Archives

Published by

The Naval & Military Press Ltd

Unit 10 Ridgewood Industrial Park,

Uckfield, East Sussex,

TN22 5QE England

Tel: +44 (0) 1825 749494

www.naval-military-press.com

www.nmarchive.com

This diary has been reprinted in facsimile from the original. Any imperfections are inevitably reproduced and the quality may fall short of modern type and cartographic standards.

© **Crown Copyright**
Images reproduced by permission of The National Archives, London, England, 2015.

Contents

Document type	Place/Title	Date From	Date To
Heading	WO95/2177/1		
Heading	23rd Division 101st Field Coy R.E. Aug 1915-1917 Oct. To Italy.		
Heading	23rd Division 101st. F.C. R.E. Vol. I. August15. Jan19		
Heading	War Diary of 101st Field Coy RE. from 25-8-15 to 31-8-15		
War Diary	Bordon Southampton.	25/08/1915	25/08/1915
War Diary	Southampton.	26/08/1915	26/08/1915
War Diary	Havre.	27/08/1915	28/08/1915
War Diary	Ganspette.	29/08/1915	31/08/1915
Miscellaneous	Appendix I. Strength of Company on Landing in France.	27/08/1915	27/08/1915
Heading	23rd Divn. 101st F.C.R.E. Vol.2. Sep15		
Heading	War Diary of 101st Field Coy R.E. from 1st September 1915 to 30th September 1915		
War Diary	Ganspette.	01/09/1915	06/09/1915
War Diary	Hazebrouck.	07/09/1915	07/09/1915
War Diary	Nota Boome.	08/09/1915	08/09/1915
War Diary	Rouge De Bout.	09/09/1915	14/09/1915
War Diary	Erquinghem.	15/09/1915	30/09/1915
Heading	23rd Division. 101st F.C.R.E. Vol.3. Oct.15		
Heading	War Diary of 101st F Coy RE from 1st Oct To 31st Oct 1915		
War Diary	Erquinghem.	01/10/1915	01/10/1915
War Diary	Beuvry.	02/10/1915	11/10/1915
War Diary	Bethune.	12/10/1915	20/10/1915
War Diary	Erquinghem.	21/10/1915	31/10/1915
Heading	23rd Division 101st R.C.R.E. Vol.4 Nov 15		
Heading	War Diary of 101st Field Company Royal Engineers from 1st November 1915 to 30th November 1915		
War Diary	Erquinghem.	01/11/1915	30/11/1915
Heading	23rd Division. 101st F.C.R.E. Vol.5		
Heading	War Diary of 101st Field Coy R.E. from 1st December 1915 to 31st December 1915		
War Diary	Erquinghem.	01/12/1915	31/12/1915
Heading	101st F.C.R.E. Vol 6. Jan 16		
Heading	War Diary of 101st Field Company R.E. from 1st January 1916 to 31st January 1916 (Volume).		
War Diary	Erquinghem.	01/01/1916	31/01/1916
Heading	War Diary of 101st Field Company Royal Engineers from 1st Feby 1916 to 29th February 1916		
Miscellaneous	A.G. G.H.Q.	01/05/1916	01/05/1916
War Diary	Erquinghem.	01/02/1916	25/02/1916
War Diary	Nouveau Monde.	26/02/1916	26/02/1916
War Diary	Nouveau Monde & Steenbecque.	27/02/1916	28/02/1916
War Diary	Steenbecque & Camblain Chapelain.	29/02/1916	29/02/1916
Heading	O i/c. A.G's Office at the Base. 101st Field Coy RE War Diary. Vol.8		
War Diary	Calonne Ricouart.	01/03/1916	12/03/1916
War Diary	Ablain St Nazaire.	13/03/1916	14/03/1916

War Diary	Ruitz.	15/03/1916	16/03/1916
War Diary	Bully-Grenay.	17/03/1916	31/03/1916
Heading	War Diary of 101st Field Company R.E. from 1st April 1916 to 30th April 1916. (Volume). Vol.9		
War Diary	Bully Grenay.	01/04/1916	30/04/1916
Heading	War Diary of 101st Field Company Royal Engineers from 1st May 1916 to 31st May 1916. (Volume). Vol.10		
War Diary	Ruitz.	01/05/1916	08/05/1916
War Diary	Bully Grenay.	09/05/1916	22/05/1916
War Diary	Bouvigny Wood.	23/05/1916	31/05/1916
Miscellaneous	D.A.G. G.H.Q 3rd Echelon.	01/07/1916	01/07/1916
Heading	War Diary of 101st Field Company Royal Engineers from 1st-30th June 1916 (Volume). Vol.11		
War Diary	Bouvigny Wood.	01/06/1916	12/06/1916
War Diary	La Thieuloye.	13/06/1916	15/06/1916
War Diary	Verchin.	16/06/1916	16/06/1916
War Diary	Mattringhem.	17/06/1916	24/06/1916
War Diary	Yzeux.	25/06/1916	30/06/1916
Heading	War Diary of 101st Field Company, R.E. From 1st July 1916 to 31st July 1916. (Volume 11). 101 F.C.R.E. Vol.12		
War Diary	Allonville.	01/07/1916	01/07/1916
War Diary	La Houssoye.	02/07/1916	02/07/1916
War Diary	Mellincourt.	03/07/1916	03/07/1916
War Diary	Albert.	04/07/1916	12/07/1916
War Diary	Franvillers.	13/07/1916	13/07/1916
War Diary	Molliens au Bois.	14/07/1916	21/07/1916
War Diary	Millencourt.	22/07/1916	26/07/1916
War Diary	Albert.	27/07/1916	27/07/1916
War Diary	Nr Shelter Wood.	25/07/1916	31/07/1916
Heading	23rd Divisional Engineers 101st Field Company R.E. August 1916		
Heading	War Diary of 101st Field Company Royal Engineers from 1st August 1916 to 31st August 1916. (Volume 12). Vol.13		
War Diary	Shelter Wood.	01/08/1916	07/08/1916
War Diary	Franvillers.	08/08/1916	09/08/1916
War Diary	Move.	09/08/1916	10/08/1916
War Diary	Coquerel.	11/08/1916	13/08/1916
War Diary	Meteren.	14/08/1916	15/08/1916
War Diary	Ploegsteert.	16/08/1916	31/08/1916
Heading	War Diary of 101st Field Company Royal Engineers from 1st September 1916 to 30th September 1916. (Volume 13). Vol.14		
War Diary	Ploegsteert.	01/09/1916	03/09/1916
War Diary	La Bourse Near Bailleul.	04/09/1916	05/09/1916
War Diary	Bleue Maison (Watten).	06/09/1916	08/09/1916
War Diary	Blue Maison.	09/09/1916	10/09/1916
War Diary	Allonville.	11/09/1916	12/09/1916
War Diary	Brestle.	13/09/1916	19/09/1916
War Diary	Becourt Wood.	20/09/1916	30/09/1916
Heading	War Diary of 101st Field Company Royal Engineers October 1st to October 31st 1916. (Volume 14). Vol.15		
War Diary	Becourt Wood.	01/10/1916	09/10/1916
War Diary	Brestle.	10/10/1916	11/10/1916
War Diary	St. Saveur.	12/10/1916	12/10/1916

War Diary	Cocquerel.	13/10/1916	14/10/1916
War Diary	Millencourt.	15/10/1916	15/10/1916
War Diary	Halifax Camp.	16/10/1916	17/10/1916
War Diary	Ypres.	18/10/1916	31/10/1916
Heading	War Diary of 101st Field Company Royal Engineers. From 1st November 1916-30th November 1916. (Volume 15). Vol.16		
War Diary	Ypres.	01/11/1916	30/11/1916
Heading	War Diary of 101st Field Coy R.E. from 1st December to 31st December 1916. (Volume No. 16). Vol.17		
War Diary	Ypres.	01/12/1916	31/12/1916
Heading	Volume 17. War Diary of 101st Field Company R.E. from January 1st 1917. to January 31st 1917		
War Diary	Ypres.	01/01/1917	31/01/1917
Heading	War Diary of 101st Field Coy R.E. from 1st February 1917 to 28th February 1917. (Volume 18). Vol.19		
War Diary	Ypres.	01/02/1917	26/02/1917
War Diary	Busseboom.	28/02/1917	28/02/1917
Heading	War Diary of 101st Field Company R.E. from March 1st 1917 to March 31st 1917 Volume 19. Vol.20		
War Diary	Herzeele Broxeele.	01/03/1917	19/03/1917
War Diary	Herzeele Houtkerque.	21/03/1917	31/03/1917
Heading	War Diary of 101st Field Company R.E. from April 1st 1917 to April 30th 1917. Volume.20. Vol.21		
War Diary	Houtkerque.	01/04/1917	06/04/1917
War Diary	Flamertinghe H.13.d.5.3	07/04/1917	30/04/1917
Heading	War Diary of 101st Field Company R.E. from May 1st 1917 to May 31st 1917. Volume 21. Vol.22		
War Diary	Vlamertinghe.	01/05/1917	02/05/1917
War Diary	Steenvoorde.	03/05/1917	05/05/1917
War Diary	G 21.a.4.4	06/05/1917	10/05/1917
War Diary	Ypres.	11/05/1917	31/05/1917
Heading	War Diary of 101st Field Company R.E. from June 1st 1917 to June 30th 1917. Volume 22. Vol.23		
War Diary	Ypres.	01/06/1917	12/06/1917
War Diary	H.13.d.3.4	13/06/1917	14/06/1917
War Diary	Bailleul.	15/06/1917	16/06/1917
War Diary	X.10.b.3.9	17/06/1917	29/06/1917
War Diary	Dickebusch.	30/06/1917	30/06/1917
Miscellaneous	Appendix A. Casualties & Honours During tour in Ypres.		
Heading	War Diary of 101st Field Company R.E. from July 1st 1917 to July 31st 1917. Volume.23. Vol.24		
War Diary	Dickebusch.	01/07/1917	31/07/1917
Heading	War Diary of 101st Field Company R.E. from August 1st 1917 to August 31st 1917. Volume 24. Vol.25		
War Diary		01/08/1917	27/08/1917
War Diary	Railway Dugouts Ypres.	28/08/1917	31/08/1917
Heading	War Diary of 101st Field Company R.E. from 1st September 1917 to 30th September 1917. Volume 25. Vol.26		
War Diary	Railway Dugouts.	01/09/1917	03/09/1917
War Diary	Berthen.	04/09/1917	23/09/1917
War Diary	Nr. Boeschepe.	24/09/1917	30/09/1917

Heading	War Diary Of 101st Field Company. R.E. From October 1st 1917. To October 31st 1917. Volume.26. Vol 27		
War Diary	Nr. Boeschepe.	01/10/1917	10/10/1917
War Diary	Chateau Segard.	11/10/1917	28/10/1917
War Diary	Boeschepe.	29/10/1917	31/10/1917

No 95/2122/1

23RD DIVISION

101ST FIELD COY R.E.

AUG 1915 - ~~JAN 1919~~
1917 OCT

TO ITALY

121/6801

23rd Division

101st F.C. R.E.
Vol I

August 15
Jan '19

Confidential

War Diary

of

101st Field Cg. R.E.

From 25-8-15 to 31-8-15.

Army Form C. 2118.

WAR DIARY
or
INTELLIGENCE SUMMARY.   101st Fd. Co. R.E.

(Erase heading not required.)

Instructions regarding War Diaries and Intelligence Summaries are contained in F. S. Regs., Part II. and the Staff Manual respectively. Title pages will be prepared in manuscript.

Place	Date 1915	Hour	Summary of Events and Information	Remarks and references to Appendices
BORDON	Aug 25		Entrained at BORDON in two equal detachments at 6.35 pm and 7.50 pm and arrived	J.C.
SOUTHAMPTON			at SOUTHAMPTON at 8.30 pm and 7.45 pm respectively.	
SOUTHAMPTON	26		Embarked in two detachments as follows.	J.C.
			2 officers 46 O.R. Vehicles and 81 horses S.S. AUSTRALIND 3.0. pm.	
			4 officers S.S. ATALANTA 6.0 pm.	
HAVRE	27		Disembarked and proceeded to No 5 Rest Camp arriving there about 7 pm. Strength as detailed in App. I	App I J.C.
			Interpreter reported for duty.	
do	28		Entrained at Quai 3 at 4.30 am and left for destination AUDRUICK.	J.C.
GANSPETTE	29		Detrained at SAINT OMER by 4.30 am and marched to GANSPETTE where company went into billets	J.C.
			C.R.E. came over to see Company.	
do	30		Route march and driving exercise. Erected water trough for Hd Qrs R.E. at TILQUES	J.C.
do	31		Route march in the morning. C.R.E. came over and inspected horses etc. Maj Gen FOWKE and	J.C.
			Col HARVEY also came over in the afternoon inspected horses it and interviewed officers.	

J.K. Armour Lt RE
Major 29.8.15
O.C. 101 [illegible]

J.J.

Army Form C.2118

WAR DIARY
INTELLIGENCE SUMMARY
(Erase heading not required)

101st Fld Co R.E.

Place	Date	Hour	Summary of Events and Information	Remarks and references to Appendices
Appx I			**APPENDIX I**	
			Strength of Company on landing in France. 27th Aug 1915.	
			Names of officers:—	
			Major I.J. Connor, R.E.	
			Capt. C.R Shannon.	
			Lieut. J.H. Heatman J/C	
			Lieut L.D.O. Hemphill, –	
			" D. Baird,	
			" J.H Henderson.	
			" A. Podmore.	
			Vehicles	
			Double Toolcart 4	
			Wagon Subsidiaries 4	
			" G.S. 1	
			" Pontoon 2	
			" Trestle 1	
			" Light Spring 1	
			" G.S. 1	
			Cart Water 1	
			Horses. 79	
			Officers 6	
			Warrant Officer 1	
			S. Sejts & Serjts 7	
			Corporals 9	
			2nd Corporals 9	
			fcc Corporals 11	
			Farrier Serjt 1	
			Sappers 138	
			Drivers 46	
			Total 228	
			Attached:	
			A.S.C. Driver 2 horses & G.S. Waggon.	
			Note 2 R.A.M.C. had not joined.	

J.J. Connor D.E.
Major
101 Fd Co R.E.
O.C. 101

8914/121

23rd Div"

101st F.C.R.E.
Vol 2

Sep 15

Confidential

WAR DIARY

of

101ˢᵗ FIELD Cᵒʸ R.E.

from 1ˢᵗ September 1915 to 30ᵗʰ September 1915.

Army Form C. 2118

WAR DIARY
or
INTELLIGENCE SUMMARY.

(Erase heading not required.)

101st Fld. Co. R.E.

Instructions regarding War Diaries and Intelligence Summaries are contained in F. S. Regs., Part II. and the Staff Manual respectively. Title pages will be prepared in manuscript.

Place	Date 1915	Hour	Summary of Events and Information	Remarks and references to Appendices
	Sept.			
GANSPETTE	1		Divisional Exercise	J.J.C.
do	2		Making Pontoon Bridge across River AA, 3 pontoons, 2 trestles, also Bridge across canal near WATTEN - 1 pontoon, 1 trestle. Rained all day. (102nd F.Co. pontoons left to us for the day).	J.J.C.
— do —	3		Rained all day. Co. fatigues + drying clothing. O.C. rode out to TRAVÈS to meet C.R.E. + discuss C.'s work on new defences.	J.J.C.
— do —	4		Major Connor, Lieuts Baird + Palmore proceeded to HQ II Corps BAILLEUL and visited trenches at ARMENTIÈRES and NEUVE EGLISE. Company cutting brushwood + making hurdles. Received orders to move by road on 6th September.	J.J.C.
— do —	5		Packing up, etc. Pontoon + trestle wagons sent to O.C. 102nd F.Co. R.E.	J.J.C.
— do —	6		Parade 5.30 am marched to HAZEBROUCK via ARQUES + ERBLINGHEM. March about 20½ miles. Billets in town. Two men left in hospital for dental treatment.	J.J.C.
HAZEBROUCK	7		Parade 9.15 am. marched to NOTA BOOME. Billeted in farmhouses. One man rejoined. Received orders to join XX Div and be attached for instruction to follows:- 2 Sect + HQ to 84th Field Co.'s Rear Rouge de Bout. 1 Sect to 83rd Co. R.E. at LAVENTIE. 1 Sect to 96th F.Co. R.E. at LAVENTIE. March about 11 miles.	J.J.C.
NOTA BOOME	8		Parade at 9.0 am. Sections marched to destinations and were billeted. Pontoon wagons empty rejoined the Co.	J.J.C.
ROUGE DE BOUT	9		Length of march HQ + 2 Sections 9 miles. Trestle wagons empty sent to join Section attached to 96th F.Co. R.E. HQ + 2 Section working on trenches. The second man left behind at HAZEBROUCK rejoined Co. O.C. went round trenches with D.C.R.E. 84th F.Co. R.E. in morning + visited out section at LAVENTIE in afternoon. 1 mule returned to No. 32 Mobile Vet. Section.	J.J.C.
— do —	10		Visited trenches in 96th F.Co. R.E. section in morning. All sections working in trenches. day work.	
— do —	11		Visited trenches in charge of 23rd F.Co. R.E. near LAVENTIE in morning.	
— do —	12		HQ + 2 Section started nightwork. Parade 5.30 pm. Remainder working on trenches as before. Received instructions from C.R.E. to proceed to ERQUINGHEM and take over from O.C. 2nd Wessex R.E.	J.J.C.

2353 Wt. W2344/1454 700,000 5/15 D.D.&L. A.D.S.S./Forms/C. 2118.

Army Form C. 2118

WAR DIARY
~~INTELLIGENCE SUMMARY~~

101st Fld Co. R.E.

(Erase heading not required.)

Instructions regarding War Diaries and Intelligence Summaries are contained in F.S. Regs., Part II. and the Staff Manual respectively. Title pages will be prepared in manuscript.

Place	Date	Hour	Summary of Events and Information	Remarks and references to Appendices
Rouge De Bout	13/9/15	8.30am	O.C. proceeded to ERQUINGHEM to Inspect Visited workshops & defences at BOIS GRENIER POST & ROLANDERIS FARM. Orders received for Co. to come to ERQUINGHEM so as to arrive on morning of 14th Sept. Pontoon wagons turned up.	J/C
"	14/9/15		Visited RUE FLEURIE & LA VESÉE POSTS. Sections of Company arrived independently. Detachment of 45 men sent to R.E. Park to supervise civilians etc.	J/C
ERQUINGHEM	15/9/15		Co. employed cleaning up billets. O.C. visited BOIS GRENIER LINE (3rd Line) Trenches with Adjt 27th Div. & took over work. Sine ex tends from BOIS GRENIER to CHAPELLE D'ARMENTIÈRES. Divisional Baths in afternoon from O.C. 2nd Wessex R.E.	J/C
— do —	16/9/15		Reported on accommodation in shelters in BOIS GRENIER LINE to C.R.E. Visited BAC ST MAUR and took over magazine containing explosives and detailed scheme for blowing up the bridge. 2nd Wessex R.E. left at 7pm. 101 F.Co. R. in reserve working on 3rd Line.	J/C
— do —	17/9/15		moved into billets occupied by 2nd Wessex R.E. Hamlet of civilians employed 181 men. BOIS GRENIER POST Commenced work on defences. Went over BOIS GRENIER LINE with C.R.E. 69th B.C.	J/C
— do —	18/9/15		Co. at work on defences. Went over BOIS GRENIER LINE to 9.S. Staffs. J/C. BOIS GRENIER POST taken over by 8th Div. Handed over portion of BOIS GRENIER Line with small parties. Erecting	J/C
— do —	19/9/15		Orders received not to work on defences during daylight except. Repairs troop at new sawing machinery in R.E. Park.	J/C
— do —	20/9/15		Attended conference of Co. 68th B.C. Discussed forthcoming operations. Erected 5 bridges on emergency roads Co. at work on defences. RUE BOITEUX. Infantry Pioneers withdrawn. 101 F. Co. Battalion 68th B.C. with Brigade.	J/C
— do —	21/9/15		Co. at work on defences night work. Visited LA VESÉE & RUE FLEURIE POSTS	J/C
— do —	22/9/15		Conference of C.O. 8th & 4th B. discussing operations. 101 F. Co. Pontoon wagons loaded up with stores	J/C
— do —	23/9/15		Co. on night work as usual. Built emergency pontoon bridge after dusk. Co. to be ready to move from 12 noon today. Called in detachments.	J/C
— do —	24/9/15		Co. standing by ready to move. Stored blankets, kits. Working party too men night work. One civilian	J/C
— do —	25/9/15		Received orders to strengthen BOIS GRENIER LINE at once. killed by splinter from a shell whilst working at LA VESÉE POST.	J/C

Army Form C. 211

WAR DIARY

or

INTELLIGENCE SUMMARY.   101st Fld C.R.E.

(Erase heading not required.)

Instructions regarding War Diaries and Intelligence Summaries are contained in F.S. Regs., Part II. and the Staff Manual respectively. Title pages will be prepared in manuscript.

Place	Date	Hour	Summary of Events and Information	Remarks and references to Appendices
ERQUINGHEM	26/9/15		Work returns to normal. Sections on night work at ROLANDERIE Farm, BOIS GRENIER LINE and LAVESEE Post.	J/C
— do —	27/9/15		Work as usual. Received orders at 11 p.m. to be ready to move tomorrow at 11 a.m. to join 19th Division.	G/C
— do —	28/9/15		Received orders at 11 p.m. to join 20th Division. Reallied eceline from nightwork. Packed up wagons & tents beforenoon. Stood (Haubst + Grafords. Reallus detachments & awaited detailed orders. About 3.30 pm orders for move were cancelled. CRE came down instructed me to hand over BOIS GRENIER LINE to 102nd FC.?	J/C
— do —	29/9/15		Handed over BOIS GRENIER LINE to OC 102nd FC. Sections on day work on roads (LAVESEE. RUE FLEURIE)	J/C
			Maj Bremner the new CRE arrived	J/C
— do —	30/9/15		old CRE left today. Co. working on trenches outpost. Received orders at 11 p.m. to be ready to move on 1st Oct. 1915. early.	J/C

J.J. Connor, Major, R.E.
O.C. 101st Fd Co R.E.

2353   Wt. W2544/1454   700,000   5/15   D.D. & L.   A.D.S.S./Forms/C. 2118.

12/
74 30

23rd Division

101st J.C.R.E.
vol 3

Oct 15

WAR DIARY
of
181st Coy. RE

From 1st Oct to 31st Oct 1915

WAR DIARY 101ª 7ª Cº R.E.

INTELLIGENCE SUMMARY.

(Erase heading not required.)

Army Form 2118.

Instructions regarding War Diaries and Intelligence Summaries are contained in F.S. Regs., Part II. and the Staff Manual respectively. Title pages will be prepared in manuscript.

Place	Date	Hour	Summary of Events and Information	Remarks and references to Appendices
ERQUINGHEM	1st Oct.		Handed over workshops, stores & defence works to 102nd & 128th T Cs. R.E. Marched to BETHUNE.	17 mile march
BETHUNE BEUVRY	2nd Oct.		and thence to BEUVRY. The company being attached to the 83rd Bde. 28th Divn. I Corp.	
			Cº on night work. Working party got shelled on way to work. Took shelter in communication trench and got mixed up with ration parties relief etc. Trenches were cleared for the attack on the HOHENZOLLERN REDOUBT. and party could not get to the site. No casualties in Cº.	
— do —	3rd.		Moved into billets at SAILLY LA BOURSE, 1 Cº on night work digging commn. Trenches & improving fire trench (BIG WILLIE). ½ Cº taking part in the attack on HOHENZOLLERN REDOUBT and wiring in front of our 1st line trenches.	
— do —	4th		Corpl Shannon C.R. was killed whilst wiring near the QUARRIES. One sapper wounded. ½ Cº wiring in front of BIG WILLIE, night work. Wire erected within 20 yds of German trenches. ½ Cº wiring in front of BIG WILLIE night work.	
— do —	5th		Returned from work 6 a.m. Marched to rest camp at GONNEHEM. (march 8 miles)	
— do —	6th		Inspection by Corps Commander. Marched 16 miles. Cleaning up billets etc.	
— do —	7th		Inspection by Corps Commander.	
— do —	8th		Routine work, drill, digging etc. 2nd Lt. Harvey joined the Cº today at 9 p.m.	
— do —	9th		— do — Lieut. Heusfield admitted to Hospital (BETHUNE).	
— do —	10th		— do — work under C.E. 1st Corps. Attached to 7th — Divn.	
— do —	11th		Cº marched to BETHUNE for work under C.E. 1st Corps. BURBURES ALLEY & Rd. (CAMBRIN)	
BETHUNE	12th		Went over defences with C.E. The Cº is to work on the 3rd line from BURBURES ALLEY to Rd. (CAMBRIN)	
— do —	13th		Cº working on defences. Work stopped at 12 noon owing to attack by XI Corps. Returns to billets. Cº working on defences.	
— do —	14th		2/ Thompson killed by fragment of shell (11" KRUPP mental) whilst returning from watering horses. Sire shells dropped in BETHUNE	
— do —	15th		a.m. night work. Working party 200 strong	
— do —	16th		— do — — do — 200 — do — ½ Cº attached to 2nd Divn for obtaining materials, tools etc. Working under C.E. 1st Corps.

2333 Wt. W2544/1454 700,000 5/15 D. D. & L. A.D.S.S./Forms/C. 2118.

WAR DIARY

Army Form C. 2118.

161st Ld. Coy. R.E.

(Erase heading not required.)

Place	Date 1915	Hour	Summary of Events and Information	Remarks and references to Appendices
BETHUNE	17th Oct.		Coy. on day work. Working party 400 men on 3rd line defences.	
do	18th "		do do do	
do	19th "		Coy. changed billets. Started to work on 3rd line defences by the	
			Received orders at 4 pm to rejoin III Corps and proceed to ERQUINGHEM. Sapr. B. Hue wounded by shrapnel (s. light).	
do	20th "		Handed over work to Maj. Wilson. 2nd Anglian Fd. Coy. R.E. Coy. marched off at 9.0 am and were inspected by Lt. Col. Saunders C.R.E. 28th Divn. before leaving. Arrived ERQUINGHEM 4 pm. March 17 miles.	
ERQUINGHEM	21st "		Unloading waggons & cleaning up billets. Started work on huts and took over part of Bois Grenier Line.	
do	22nd "		Making dug out frames, French ladders etc. Inspected 3rd line and portion of 1st line near Salient.	
do	23rd "		Capt. O.C. 107th 13th R.F.A. choosing gun positions for gun emplacements in Bois Grenier near Salient etc. Coy. working as yesterday.	
do	24th "		Inspected approaches to guns & getting out details for bridges. Took over work over gun emplacements from 128th Coy.	
do	25th "		Marking out positions of gun emp. Lieut. Nigel George Compton R.E. (T.C.) joined the Coy today.	
do	26th "		Working on gun emplacements etc.	
do	27th "		do do	
do	28th "		do do Lines of fire were changed today by the Staff. This will mean new gun emplacements in different positions.	
do	29th "		Met O.C. 107th 13th R.F.A. to discuss new arrangements.	
do	30th "		Working on gun emplacements etc	
do	31st "		do	

J.J. O'Connor
Major R.E.
O.C. 161st L. Coy. R.E.

10125 F.C.R.E.
vol: 4

12/7724

23rd Atvraun

Nov. 15

Confidential

War Diary
of
101st Field Company,
Royal Engineers

From 1st November 1915 to 30th November 1915.

J. Connor
Major, R.E.
Commanding 101st Field Co.

Army Form C. 2118.

WAR DIARY
INTELLIGENCE SUMMARY.

101st Field Coy. R.E.
November 1915

(Erase heading not required.)

Instructions regarding War Diaries and Intelligence Summaries are contained in F. S. Regs., Part II. and the Staff Manual respectively. Title pages will be prepared in manuscript.

Place	Date 1915	Hour	Summary of Events and Information	Remarks and references to Appendices
ERQUINGHEM	1-Nov			
	2nd Nov		Work on gun emplacement 2 18pr guns & 1 mountain gun. 1 Section on hutting. Civilians on digging trenches & revetting. BOIS GRENIER LINE. Making trench ladders, filling knife rests and dug out frames in workshops.	
do	3rd Nov		do	
do	4th Nov		do	
do	5th Nov		Work as above.	
			Draft of seven men (reinforcements) joined the Coy.	
do	6th Nov		Lt. N.G. CROMPTON was shot through the heart & died practically instantaneously whilst carrying up stores to the 18pr gun emplacement, at about 100 yards from the railway dump.	
do	7th Nov		Work as usual.	
do	8th Nov		No work today. Lt. NIGEL GEORGE CROMPTON was buried today at 3.30 p.m. in the military Cemetery at ERQUINGHEM SUR LYS.	
			Nos 1,3 & 4 Sections hutting. No 2 Section hutting.	
do	9th		do	
do	10th		do	Buflected 18pr gun empl't approved work with Lt. J.F. LINNEHAN? Hut R. Pr. repairs to Bde CRENIER Line joining Pre Bn? Trenches 2 Day & 3 night.
do	11th		do	
do	12th		do	
do	13th		do	
do	14th		do	Buflected 18pr gun empl't approved work.
do	15th		Work as last week. Huts on new site at LA ROLANDERIE commenced. 3 new shelters 2ft? Wide 9? office.	
do	16th		do	
do	17th			
do	18th		Working on hutting. 40 huts at Fort Rompu Sides & weather boarded	
do	19th			J.C.

2353   Wt. W2544/1454 700,000 5/15   D. D. & L.   A.D.S.S./Forms/C. 2118.

Army Form C. 2118

WAR DIARY

Confidential

INTELLIGENCE SUMMARY.
(Erase heading not required.)

101st Field Coy. RE.
November 1915.

Place	Date	Hour	Summary of Events and Information	Remarks and references to Appendices
ERQUINGHEM 1915	20th		Coy on hutting. Work on huts in FORT ROMPU area. Finished 12 huts to-day. 1 Section on BOIS GRENIER LINE reconstructing trenches and making dug-out shelters.	
— do —	21st		Fatigues, checking stores etc.	
— do —	22nd		Coy working on hutting (3 sections). 1 Section on BOIS GRENIER LINE	
— do —	23rd		— do — — do —	
	24th		— do — — do —	
	25th		— do — — do — (12 huts finished).	
	26th			
	27th		Started work on huts in JESUS FARM area — do —	
	28th		Work on huts. 2 sections. 1 Section on water supply to front line. 1 Section reconstructing S.S. in Trenches	
	29th		— do — — do —	
	30th		Draft of 6 men joined the Coy. To-day. Work as yesterday. 12 more huts finished.	

L. J. Connor
Major RE.
O.C. 101:

23rd K. Warden.

101 X Police.
Wt. 5

121/7911

Secret
Confidential

War Diary
of
101st Field Coy. R.E.

from 1st December 1915 to 31st December 1915.

Army Form C. 2118.

WAR DIARY
INTELLIGENCE SUMMARY. 101st Field Co. R.E.

December 1915.

(Erase heading not required.)

Place	Date	Hour	Summary of Events and Information	Remarks and references to Appendices
ERQUINGHEM	1st Dec.		2 Sections hutting at JESUS FARM area. 1 Section on water supply to front line. 1 Section in Bois GRENIER Line reconstructing trenches.	
	2nd Dec.		Lieut Baird went on 10 days leave	
	3rd		Work as yesterday. 11 huts completed.	
	4th		— do —	
	5th		— do — 6 huts completed.	
			Fatigues. Sapper Duncan 45378 to proceed to No 4 Gen Base Depot for duty w/R.E Base Parks. No 63717 Sapr Hadlow proceeded to BETHUNE for duty at 1st Army Bomb Factory. Hutting started in HALLOBEAU area.	
	6th		Work as last week. R. LYS very high. Banks flooded. 7 huts completed.	
	7th		— do — 7 huts — do —	
	8th		— do — 4 huts — do —	
	9th		— do — ERQUINGHEM shelled by Germans today. 30 shells 5.9 fell in the village. No (657?) Sapr Evans wounded in right shoulder by H.E m.B.G. line.	
	10th		— do — No (657?) Sapr ———	
	11th		— do — 13 huts completed.	
	12th		Still raining. R. LYS rising. Large portion of yard flooded out. Lieut Hargreaves went on leave.	
	13th		Inspected BRIDOUX SALIENT and RETRENCHMENT with C.R.E. Trenches all fallen in. Coy. on fatigues &c. No 1 Section on water supply to BRIDOUX SALIENT. No 2 & 3 Sec. on reconstructing trenches in BRIDOUX SALIENT. No 4 Sect reconstructing trenches BOIS GRENIER LINE.	
	14th		RETRENCHMENT. 1 Sect. No 3 on hutting. Civilians on making hand wires &c.	
	15th		— do —	
	16th		— do — Sapr Pagg suffering from shock H.E. shell shelled the Bois GRENIER BRIDOUX SALIENT Rd.	
	17th		— do —	
	18th		— do —	
	19th		Actg. my. Raines Paid C. Court of Inquiry on two bicycles lost.	

Army Form C. 2118.

WAR DIARY

INTELLIGENCE SUMMARY.

(Erase heading not required.)

101st Field Coy RE
December 1915.

Place	Date	Hour	Summary of Events and Information	Remarks and references to Appendices
ERQUINGHEM	20/12		Coy on same work as last week. Raining	
do	21st		do	
do	22nd		do	
do	23rd		do — River LYS flooded its banks nearly over road.	No
do	24th		do	
do	25th		do	
do	26th		Fatigues, stocking parks.	
do	27th		Coy on same work as last week.	
do	28th		do — Sapr. Molin (N° 57857) wounded in right shoulder by rifle bullet whilst working at BRIDOUX SALIENT Retrenchment.	
do	29th		do — Fine. Made out schemes for destruction of bridges over R. LYS at BAC ST NAUR and ERQUINGHEM. Also for destruction of ERQUINGHEM church tower and culvert on road at H.9.d 10.8. Sheet 36 NW. 1/20,000	
do	30th		do — Fine.	
do	31st		do — Lt. Pomeroe went on leave.	

N Connor
Major RE
O.C. 101 Field Coy RE

101st S. C. T. E.

Vot. 6
Tau 716

23

Confidential

War Diary
of
101st Field Company, R.E.

from 1st January 1916, to 31st January 1916.
(Volume   )

[Signature]
Major, R.E.
Commanding 101st Field Co., R.E.

WAR DIARY or INTELLIGENCE SUMMARY

Army Form C. 2118.

167 ?? Corps RE

January 1916.

Place	Date	Hour	Summary of Events and Information	Remarks and references to Appendices
ERQUINGHEM	1st Jan.		No.1 Sec. water supply to BRIDOUX SALIENT and bomb stores (B).	
do	2nd Jan		No.2 Sec. N.F. & No.3 on reconstructing trenches BRIDOUX SALIENT RETRENCHMENT.	
do	3rd		Left ½ Sec. No.3 on hutting started at ROLANDERIE today.	
do	4th		No.4 Section reconstructing trenches of BOIS GRENIER LINE.	
do	5th		Fatigue. Bathing parade. Paid Cg "H"	
do	6th		Work as detailed above.	
do	7th		do	
do	8th		do Sapr Mackie (No 1496) wounded in the neck in BRIDOUX SALIENT.	
do	9th		do	
do	10th		do Started work on two observation posts for R.F.A. at T.19.c.9.6. & I.14.b.4.h.	
do	11th		do Started work on hut at RUE DELETTRE.	
do	12th		Fatigues do Kit inspection. Gas helmet drill. Lieut. Powers returned from leave.	
do	13th		Work as for last week.	
do	14th		do Started work on huts at RUE DES ACQUETS.	
do	15th		do	
do	16th		do Started work on hut at RUE DORMOIRE.	
do	17th		do Major Cruer went for week's leave to England. Works Office on O.P. at Mose Farm moving to Fleurbaix	N.C.
do	18th		do Fatigues. Rifle & Kit inspection. Gas helmet drill. Paid Cg.	
do	19th		do Work on new O.P. at MOAT FARM begun.	
do	20th		do Sapper Derbyshire (No 53045) shot himself. Sergt Nightingale (No 46725) slightly wounded by shell of enemy in Bois Grenier line.	N.C.

Army Form C. 2118.

101st F.C. O.B. R.E.

WAR DIARY
INTELLIGENCE SUMMARY.
(Erase heading not required.)

January 1916.

Place	Date	Hour	Summary of Events and Information	Remarks and references to Appendices
ERQUINGHEM	22nd Jan.		Work as detailed. No. 48211 Sapr Jenkins wounded in hand & thigh by rifle bullet in BRIDOUX Salient.	J.C.
— do —	23rd		Major Connor returned to duty from leave. Fatigues. Kit inspection & Gas helmet drill.	
— do —	24th		No. 1 Sec. on water supply to BRIDOUX SALIENT, Bomb store and alterations at E.F.F. Cruttur. No. 2 Sec. reconstructing BRIDOUX SALIENT and RETRENCHMENT. ½ No. 3 Sec. lying No. 2 Sect. ½ No. 3 Sec. with 20 Inf. in hutting 16th 17th B. B. Transport Lines. Also making amm. slides for 102nd Amm. Col. 103rd Amm. Col. 105th Amm. Col & 104th Amm. Col. No. 4 Sect. reconstructing BOIS GRENIER LINE. H.Q. Section working in workshops.	
— do —	25th		H.Q. & 3 Sections on O.P. at Mast Farm and near ESTAMINET. 2nd Lt. Harvey R.E. went on leave. (H.Q. & 2 Sec.)	
— do —	26th		— do — Lieut Col. R.E. billeted in our factory not attached to for work. O.C. J. Major McMahon (T.C.) R.E.	
— do —	27th		— do — Germans shelled right of BRIDOUX SALIENT very heavily several direct hits on dugouts & parapets. Sapr Blackburn (No. 6584) wounded in back by splinter. No. 13972 Sapr Nelson wounded in L hand & thigh by shell splinter whilst on BGline work. Order 440 O.C. 207/328 and points out work to be done.	J.C.
— do —	28th		Sect. 207 F.C. O.B. R.E. attached to us started work on BOIS GRENIER LINE. Repairing damages caused by shell fire etc.	
— do —	29th		— do —	
— do —	30th		Pay of Cd. Kit inspection. Gas helmet drill. Fatigues.	
— do —	31st		Work as detailed for last week. Commenced work on hooures O.P. for R.F.A. Draft of 4 men reinforcements arrived to Coy.	

J. Connor
Major R.E.
OC 101 F.C. O.B. R.E.
2/2/16

Confidential

War Diary

of

101st Field Company, Royal Engineers

from 1st Feby 1916 to 29th February 1916.

A.G.
G.H.Q.
―――

I enclose herewith the original of my war diary for 1st Feb. 12th Feb. 1916 inclusive which I have just discovered. It was apparently not sent with the diary for the remainder of the month through an oversight which is regretted.

J.J. O'Connor
Major, R.E.
Commanding 101st Field Co. R.E.

1 5/16.

Confidential.

WAR DIARY

INTELLIGENCE SUMMARY.
(Erase heading not required.)

February 1916.

101st 2/0 (S) RE

Army Form C. 2118.

Instructions regarding War Diaries and Intelligence Summaries are contained in F.S. Regs., Part II. and the Staff Manual respectively. Title pages will be prepared in manuscript.

Place	Date	Hour	Summary of Events and Information	Remarks and references to Appendices
ERQUINGHEM	1st Feb.		Nos 1 & 2 sections reconstructing trenches in BRIDOUX SALIENT and laying in water supply. No 3 section hutting. Finished ammunition shelter for Aus. CE.	
do	2nd Feb		No 4 " reconstructing trenches BOIS GRENIER LINE, S.A.A store & A&P 13th Hd. dugout	J.C.
do	3rd Feb		2 Sections 207th D. Coy R.E. drawing trenches & putting up trenchgrids in BOIS GRENIER LINE. A new O.P. for R.F.A. being constructed under Lt. Ridgewell for over payment of all civilians employed by us.	J.C.
do	4th "		do	
do	5th "		All civilians handed over to O/c Labour Corps who engages them. Work of civilians proceeding as before. 2nd Lt. Luichau proceeded on leave.	
do	6th "		do	
do	7th "		do	
do	8th "		Massage Day, Bathing parade, kit inspection fatigues. Work as for last week.	
do	9th "		MINOR 2nd Lt Harvey granted extension of leave to 15th Feb. on med. Cert.	
do	9th "		Capt O'Donnell wounded by shrapnel in foot not serious. Sergt Foster knocked down by wounded man shoulder broken serious.	
do	10th "		Commenced work on new post on W. E face of Bois Grenier Pot. Two casualties Sergt Young & Pte Bresherent.	
do	11th "		Per billet was shelled. Three horses slightly hit. Removed horse lines to Hallobeau. wounded.	
do	12th "		Germans shelled BRIDOUX SALIENT very heavily. Corporal E.G. Abherley badly wounded.	J.C.

Army Form C. 2118.

WAR DIARY
or
INTELLIGENCE SUMMARY.
(Erase heading not required.)

101st Field Co RE
February 1916.

Instructions regarding War Diaries and Intelligence Summaries are contained in F.S. Regs., Part II. and the Staff Manual respectively. Title pages will be prepared in manuscript.

Place	Date	Hour	Summary of Events and Information	Remarks and references to Appendices
ERQUINGHEM	13th Feb 1916		Paid Coys. Kit inspections. Fatigues etc. Man going Coys. as trench pioneers etc.	
	14th Feb 1916		No 1 & 2 Sections work on BRIDOUX SALIENT. Advance Party from 209th F.Co. R.E. arrived today. No 3 Section working on Latrines. No 4 on Bois Grenier line. HQ section in workshops. Repairs to Bac St Maur bridge and dug out for the 26th Field Ambulance. Advanced Major Drew O.C. 209th F.Co. came out to see us.	
	15th		Reinforcement of 7 men joined Coy. 2 Lt Linehan returned from leave. Capt Brooke Coy 209th F.Co. R.E. came down. Was shown round works.	
	16th		Work as usual. { 2 Lt B.B. Harvey R.E. struck off strength of Coy. as unfit for General Service. Authority 3rd Corps A/577/16 dated 14.2.16. Authority A 480/152 dated 24.2.16. 3rd Corps A/577/16 dated 14.7.16 ? Div. d A.+ A+ H.Q, and 23rd Div. } joined party 209th F.Co. R.E.	
	17th		2 Lt Key relieved Lt. Ost of Advance Party 209th F.Co. R.E. Started work on new huts at Rue de Lettree. Received orders to move to Nouveau Monde in 24th Feb. to work under C.R.E. 3rd Corps.	
	18th	do		
	19th	do	2nd Lt Shaw R.E. (William Lindsay) T.C. joined for duty in place of 2 Lt Harvey	
	20th	do		
	21st	do	Lieut Passmore & advance party of 8 O.R. proceeded to NOUVEAU MONDE	
	22nd		to take over work from 209th F.Co. R.E. and get ready for arrival of 101st F.Co. R.E. in 24th inst. Roge over & inspected work at Nouveau Monde.	
	23rd			
	do		Finished new huts at Rue de Lettree. Also Latrines at Jesus Farm. Works Ele Huts and then packed wagons & cleaned up billets. Orders to move to Nouveau Monde were cancelled.	
	24th		Packed up wagons etc, and awaited orders. Red orders to move to NOUVEAU MONDE in 25th inst.	
	25th		Moved off at 8 am via Croix du Bac, SAILLY arrived NOUVEAU MONDE at 10.45 am. Co. getting settled in billets	

2353 Wt. W2544/1454 700,000 5/15 D.D. & L. A.D.S.S./Forms/C. 2118.

Army Form C. 2118.

101st S.O.B.? R.E.
February 1916

WAR DIARY
INTELLIGENCE SUMMARY.
(Erase heading not required.)

Instructions regarding War Diaries and Intelligence Summaries are contained in F.S. Regs., Part II. and the Staff Manual respectively. Title pages will be prepared in manuscript.

Place	Date	Hour	Summary of Events and Information	Remarks and references to Appendices
NOUVEAU MONDE	26th Feb		Co. under direct orders of C.E. 3rd Corps. 1 Section at work on bridge over R.Lys at MAISON ROUGE. Remainder of Co. on fatigues. Orders from C.R.E. 23rd Divn. to standfast. Rec'd orders from 23rd Divn. at 3.30 p.m. to march with 69th Bde. to rest area in the 27th Feb 1915. Starting point L 13 b 26. 101st G.Co. to hand over this point at 11.36 a.m.. 2 no Lt. John Stephen Burns R.E. (T.C.) (date of commission 12-11-15. date of arrival in France 22/1/16) joined the company for duty to-day.	N.C.
— do — STEENBECQUE	27th		Co. in billets. Le Paro. arrived about 3.30 p.m. Marched to STEENBECQUE via NEUF BERQUIN, VIERHOUK, Co. billeted in farms rather scattered.	
— do —	28th		Co. in billets, cleaning up billets, making latrines etc. Received orders to pack up and be ready to start for an unknown destination. Co. to go by train. Point of entrainment CALONNE RICOUART. Billeting party of 1 Off'r & 1 N.R. to proceed by motor ambulance leaving 7 a.m. to be followed by 1st train. arrive CALONNE RICOUART 11.30 a.m. Much delay in entraining being charged of to trains being ordered. Galists starting owing to order of entraining being changed & to trains being ordered. Galists had to proceed by road. No arrangements to be to meet us, the letting parties had to come by train as no motor ambulance was available. Got fixed up in billets at about 3 p.m.	
— do — CAMBLAIN CHAPELAIN	29"		Wagons etc arrived at 7.30 p.m. 500 men reinforcements arrived today.	

J. Connor
Major R.E.
O.C. 101st S.Co. R.E.

2353 Wt. W2544/1454 700,000 5/15 D.D. & L. A.D.S.S./Forms/C. 2118.

Confidential

O/c
A.G's Office at the Base.
101st Field Coy RE
War Diary.

Army Form C. 2118.

WAR DIARY
or
INTELLIGENCE SUMMARY.
(Erase heading not required.)

101st Field Coy RE
March 1916.

Place	Date	Hour	Summary of Events and Information	Remarks and references to Appendices
CALONNE-RICOUART	1st March	—	Co. getting settled into billets. Refitting. Clearing harness etc.	
	2nd	—	do Paid Company.	
	3rd	—	do	
	4th	—	Snowing hard. Lectures to men in billets. Stuff still & muskety. CRE & DC Cy. visits French trenches at SOUCHEZ held by 17th Fus. Bn. 6th Bde. RE Fres. trench.	
	5th	—	All officers attending lecture by Corps Commander at BRUAY at 3 pm.	
	6th	—	Fatigues.	
	7th	—	O.C. visited Gov. SERVINS (RE Dump) and ABLAIN ST NAZAIRE to see billets. Paid Company.	
	7th	—	Co. marched to ABLAIN ST NAZAIRE via DIVIONS, FRESNICOURT, GOUY-SERVINS. Left 2pm arrived 9.30pm. Billeted in dugouts. HO & mounted section billets at GOUY-SERVINS	
	8th	—	Settling into billets. All dugouts flooded out and had to be pumped out. Rearranging & fitting accommodation with Gen. Const. 69th Bde.	
	9th	—	Visited trenches with Brig. Gen. 69th B.C. arranging about advanced RE Dumps.	
	10th	—	Right & Centre Sectors allotted to 101st & 9th Co. RE. Brigade relief tonight no work done. Cannot work by day. Trenches very wet due to bad condition. Drainage, trench boards, revetting & provision of dugouts necessary.	
	11th	—	All sections out on night work as above. Work handicapped by want of stores.	
	12th	—	Nos 3 & 4 Sections on night work. Nos 1 & 2 sections probing up getting ready for moving to RUITZ tomorrow. CRE's Op. Order N°5.	1/O

Army Form C. 2118.

WAR DIARY
or
INTELLIGENCE SUMMARY.
(Erase heading not required.)

101st Field Coy RE

March 1916.

Place	Date	Hour	Summary of Events and Information	Remarks and references to Appendices
ABLAIN ST NAZAIRE	13th March		Nos 1 & 2 Sections under command of 2nd Lieuten RE proceeded to RUITZ at 8.30am to report to O.C. 4th London FCo RE on arrival. 2nd/Lt Burns RE joined this party at GOUY SERVINS. Route GOUY SERVINS, HERSIN. (3 officers 7 s OR) Nos 3 & 4 Section working on drainage of fire trenches in right and centre section of our line mg from BOYAU D'ERSATZ to BOYAU 130 km Brit. inclusive.	J.C. (1 kinsman)
— '' —	14th March		HQ & Nos 3 & 4 Sections relieved by 4th London FCo RE. HQ etc 101st FCo RE marched out 6.30am & proceeded to RUITZ with GOUY SERVINS, PETIT SERVINS, GRAND SERVINS, HERSIN, BARLIN, MAISNIL LES RUITZ, RUITZ. Arrived 2 pm. Settling into billets. Received reinforcements of 3 men.	
RUITZ	15th March		Fatigues on billets. O.C. went round new work with CRE 2nd Div & CRE 23rd Div. Cos to be employed on work on the LE MAISTRE LINE (3rd Line) from the Railway Point M.9 a.9.1. to Point R.23 c.2.5. Sheet 36c. Scale 1 to 10,000. Trenches in bad condition no revetting, no firesteps, no traverses in poor condition. No trench boards. Very few dug outs. Soil blue river chalk.	
— do —	16th	—	Co marched into BULLY GRENAY arriving there about 7 p.m. Billets were not fixed up by 6th Lt Col Bde and had some trouble getting on. Mounted section & transport billeted at SAINS EN GOHELLE with Capt Buckingham held bay. (Buckenham) Setting settled into billets. Went round the whole line of trenches with Capt Walker RE 1st Sect Hughes 9 O.C. RE. In afternoon saw Capt Taylor O.C. "B" Co 9th S. Staff. and allotted work as follows. No day work possible. Working hours 6 pm to 4 am. RE to work from Railway near Zone 11 to the right 9th S. Staff to work from AIX NOULETTE SOUCHEZ road to the left. Each section or platoon to commence work at the head of a communication trench and to work outwards.	B. B.
Bullion BULLY-GRENAY	17th	—		
— do —	18th		Went round line of trenches with Capt Taylor O.C. "B" Co "B" g 9th S. Staff inspected work done. made arrangements for transport and stores. Rode over to SAINS EN GOHELLE to see CRE 2nd Div about details of work.	
— do —	19th		Saffon Buckingham sentenced by F.G.C.M. to 28 days F.P.No1 for drunkenness. Confirmed 16 3/16. Promulgated 19-3-16. (7-3-16).	M.C.

2353 Wt. W2544/1454 700,000 5/15 D. D. & L. A.D.S.S./Forms/C. 2118.

WAR DIARY
INTELLIGENCE SUMMARY.
(Erase heading not required.)

Army Form C. 2118.

101st Field Co. RE

March 1916.

Place	Date	Hour	Summary of Events and Information	Remarks and references to Appendices
BULLY GRENAY	20th March		All sections on night work on LE MAISTRE LINE. Also "B" Coy. 9th S. Staffs Regt.	
do	21st		do — Reinforcement 1 man received.	
do	22nd		do — Infantry working party 400 men did not turn up	
do	23rd		do — 400 men worked 5 p.m. to 2 a.m.	N/A
do	24th		do — do	
do	25th		do — do	
do	26th		do — reported for work but was recalled by orders of Div. owing to wet weather	
do	27th		do — Infantry working party cancelled owing to wet weather	
do	28th		do — Working party 400 men on Maistre Line	
do	29th		do — 300 men — do	
do	30th		do — 350 " — do	
do	31st		do — do	

N.J. Connor
Major RE
101st Fd Co. RE

101FE RE
vol 9

XXIII

Confidential

War Diary
of
181st Field Company. R.E.

From 1st April 1916 to 30th April 1916.

(Volume)

WAR DIARY
INTELLIGENCE SUMMARY
(Erase heading not required.)

Army Form C. 2118.

101st Field Co. R.E.
April 1916.

Place	Date	Hour	Summary of Events and Information	Remarks and references to Appendices
Bully Grenay	1st April 1916		All sections on night work. Reconstructing Le Maistre line. Inf. working party 350 men.	
	2nd		do	
	3rd		do	
	4th		Formed a fifth (H.Q.) section for work on LE MAISTRE LINE under 2nd Lt. Berne	
	5th		Nos 2, 3, 4 Sections started work on BATAILLE LINE on right flank of divisional area. Working party 200 men	
	6th		No 1 and H.Q. Sections on Maistre line. Working party 100 men. On Maistre line 180 men.	
	7th		Work as above. Inf. working party on Bataille line 250 men.	
	8th		do	
	9th		do	
	10th		do	
	11th		Major Conner went on leave tonight (16th–18th). Inf. working parties 250 on Bat. All. Line 150 on Maistre line. Staffed work on Machine gun emplt No 243. Started work on Machine gun emplt No 9410.	
	12th		do	
	13th		do	All leave cancelled
	14th		do	
	15th		All officers men recalled from leave. Work as usual. Major Conner R.E. returned from leave.	No 3 Sec under Lt Henderson proceed to PERNES for duty with Commandant IV Corps School.
	16th		do	
	17th			

V.J.C.

Army Form C. 2118.

101st Field Bn. R.E.
April 1916.

WAR DIARY
INTELLIGENCE SUMMARY.
(Erase heading not required.)

Instructions regarding War Diaries and Intelligence Summaries are contained in F.S. Regs., Part II. and the Staff Manual respectively. Title pages will be prepared in manuscript.

Place	Date	Hour	Summary of Events and Information	Remarks and references to Appendices
Bully-Grenay	18th April 1916		Handed over work on Maistre Line to O.C. 226th F. Co. R.E. C. B. at work on Bajolle Line. Inf. working party 300 men.	
do	19th		Went round Bajolle Line with O.C. 222nd F. Co. R.E. 1 Sect. 226th F. Co. R.E. working with Co. on Bajolle Line. Infantry working party 300 men.	
do	20th		Work as yesterday. Inf. working party 300 men. Rained all day & night.	
do	21st		Heavy rain interfered with work. No work done.	
do	22nd		do	
do	23rd		Inf. working party cancelled.	
do	24th		Co. marched into rest at RUITZ via SAINS EN GOHELLE, HERSIN, BARLIN. Left 7.30am arrived 9.45pm	
do	25th		Co. refitting equipment etc. Lieut D. Baird acting as Adjutant R.E.	J.C.
do	26th		do Co. marched to LE VIELFORT to attend gas demonstration	
do	27th		Squad & Section drill. Six men working at No. 22 Casualty Clearing Station Bruay. 1 Lt Burns with No. 4 Section relieved No. 3 Section under Lt. Henderson at Corps School PERNES. No. 3 section returned to rest at RUITZ. Lieut. Henderson stayed behind to hand over work.	
do	28th		Physical drill, section drill etc. Lieut Henderson reported for duty.	
do	29th		No. 1 Section erecting hut for 70th Fd Ambulance. Remainder section drill, musketry etc.	
do	30th		Company went to Froze No. 7 Barlin and got bathed. Easter Day.	

J. J. Connor
Major R.E.
O.C. 101 Fd Co R.E.

1st FEB
Vol 10
XXIII

Confidential
War Diary
of

101st Field Company, Royal Engineers

from 1st May 1916. to 31st May 1916.

(Volume)

Army Form C. 2118.

WAR DIARY
or
INTELLIGENCE SUMMARY.

(Erase heading not required.)

107th F.C. R.E.
May 1916.

Place	Date	Hour	Summary of Events and Information	Remarks and references to Appendices
Ruitz	1st May 1916		No.1 Section proceeded to VILLERS SUR BOIS reporting for duty to O.C. 2/3 London Field Coy. R.E. via Barlin, Hersin. Grand Section leaving here at 4.45 p.m. (attached July 47th Div.) Mounted portion of Company wagons etc marched to Fosse 10 leaving here at 2 p.m. & took over billets from 102nd F.Coy. R.E. H.Q. of Company & Nos 2 & 3 sections marched to BULLY GRENAY leaving here 5.15 p.m. and took over work from 102nd F.Coy. R.E. No.4 Section will rejoin the company on the evening of 3rd May.	
do	2nd May		Half of No.3 Section on sanitary work in Tilleuls. No.2 Section & half No.3 with working party of 100 infantry on Bajolle Line R.36.a. Lieut Henderson went on leave tonight.	
do	3rd May		do 1st Lt Barnes & No.4 Section rejoined Company. Went round with O/C RE 2nd Div (Lt Col Brown) to find junction of M2 (Maistre Line) with 47th Div Lootour way on Lorette Spur.	
do	4th		Work as before. Drove to Div HQ with O/C RE 2nd Div to see CE and thence to CRE 47th Div. Decided about M2 and where we should start work. (R.35.c.5.)	
do	5th		Work as before. No Inf. working parties available. 1st Lt Burnes with No.4 section started work on Le Maistre Line M2 on extreme right flank of division. (R.35.c.5.)	
do	6th		Work as yesterday. Working party of 100 Inf. 1/D Company 9th S. Staffs commenced work on Le Maistre Line M2 at point R.29.c.8.5.	
do	7th		Work as yesterday. Paid Company	
do	8th		do Lieut Baird returned for duty with Company.	

Lieut-Baird returned for duty with Company.

JMC

WAR DIARY
INTELLIGENCE SUMMARY.
(Erase heading not required.)

Army Form C. 2118.

101st Field Coy R.E.
May 1916.

Place	Date	Hour	Summary of Events and Information	Remarks and references to Appendices
Bully Grenay	9th May		Nos 3 & 4 and H.Q. No 2 Section on night work. Left ½ No 2 Section day work. No 1 Sec. attached to duty with 2/3 London Field Coy R.E. 47th Divn. Nos 2 & 3 Sections working on Bajolle Line R 36 a 5.5. with 50 Inf working party. No 4 Section on Maistre Line M2 at R 35 c 5.1. with 50 Infantry — "D" "B" "J" "S" Staffs working on Maistre line at R 29 c 6.5.	
do	10th May		Work as usual. Working party 200 Inf. half on Bajolle Line + half on Maistre line. Ruined most of the night. Went round Maistre line with O.C.R.E. 2nd Divn	
do	11th May		Work as usual. No Infantry working parties	
do	12th "		do	
do	13th "		do (Lieut. D. Baird went on 8 days leave to England. Company went to Bois Bethonsay.	J.C.
do	14th "		Work as usual Nos 2 & 3 on night work. No 4 on day work. Working party 250 infantry Working party 220 Infantry	
do	15th "		do — Bajelle Line.	
do	16th "		Sergt Allum wounded in the leg whilst working on Bajelle Line. Work as usual. Working party 200 Infantry. Lieut Girondin returned from leave. Went with O.C.R.E. 23rd Divn to see O.R.E. 47th Divn and to take over new sector from 1/3 London F.Coy R.E. and company 4 R.W.F. Pioneers.	J.C.
do	17th "		Nos 2 & 3 sections squaring up & returning life. No 4 Section marched to Bouvigny Wood. Getting camp ready for company H.Q. wagons left 7.30pm. Marched to Bouvigny Wood	
do	18th "		No 2 Section marched off 10 am. No 3 Section left 2.30pm.	
do	19th "		Company hutting ad making officers latrines etc. No 4 Section working on H2.	
do	20th "		do	
do	21st "		No 2 Sec de Lorette & camp shelled with tear shell. Relief going on trenches. Put the whole company into dug cave. No work done.	
do	22nd "		Working party 200 men. Work done on Bajelle & Bajelle Switch Line and communication trenches leading up to them. Attack of 1.30 the shelled with tear shells. Much difficulty in getting W.P. through life.	

Army Form C. 2118.

WAR DIARY
of 101st Field Coy R.E.

INTELLIGENCE SUMMARY.
May 1916.

(Erase heading not required.)

Instructions regarding War Diaries and Intelligence Summaries are contained in F. S. Regs., Part II. and the Staff Manual respectively. Title pages will be prepared in manuscript.

Place	Date	Hour	Summary of Events and Information	Remarks and references to Appendices
Bouvigny Wood	23rd May.1916		Lt. Baird returned from leave. Co. working on Bayolle Line, Bayolle-Sartel Line, Dugouts for M.G. detachments, communication trenches to Bayolle line. Water supply in Bouvigny wood. No. 1, 2 & 4 night work No 3 day work. Visual signalling post on North Dume de Lorette put in. Working party 357 men. 1st Worcester Regt.	J.C.
do	24th		Work as above. 300 men " "	
do	25th		Battalion relief, no work done.	
do	26th		Work as for 24th Working party 300 men 1st Worcester Regt.	
do	27th		do 300 do	
do	28th		do 300 do	2nd Lt. Burns went to hospital J.C.
do	29th		do 200 do 150 men 10th N.F.	
10/27/13MM			CRE informed me that Capt Gardiner with A Co. No 11 Trenching Battn would report to me for work on communication trenches. Sent Peguero refused from leave.	J.C.
do	30th		Battalion Relief. no work done in Bayolle Line.	
do	31st		Co. ordered to move camp to X 1 a 6.3. and transport lines move to Bois D'OLHAIN Q 14 d 6.8. Did not complete move till after midnight. No working parties.	

J.J. Queex Major R.E.
O.C. 101st F.Co. R.E.

2353. Wt. W2544/1454. 700,000 5/15. D. D. & L. A.D.S.S./Forms/C. 2118c.

WD/46

D.A.G.
G.H.Q 3rd Echelon.

Herewith enclosed
Original War Diary of this
unit for the month of
June 1916.

J.J. Connor
Major, R.E
Commanding 101st Field Co. R.E.

1 7/16.

June
101 F C R E
Vol II

War Diary

of

151st Field Company - Royal Engineers

from 1st - 30th June 1916

(Volume XXIII)

Army Form C. 2118.

WAR DIARY
107th Field Coy. R.E.

INTELLIGENCE SUMMARY.
June 1916.

(Erase heading not required.)

Instructions regarding War Diaries and Intelligence Summaries are contained in F.S. Regs., Part II. and the Staff Manual respectively. Title pages will be prepared in manuscript.

Place	Date	Hour	Summary of Events and Information	Remarks and references to Appendices
Bouzincourt Woods	1st June 1916		Company getting settled into camp. Making cookhouses, latrines, shelters etc. No working parties.	J.C.
do	2nd		# Working Party 200 men. 10th W. Riding D.Coy. 9" S. Staff. 2 platoons 'A'Coy N°11 Rot. Batt" working on Bazin de Sapraix. N°s 1, 2, 3, 4 sections working on Bazille & Bazille-Warte lines and on making deep dug-outs for machine gun detachments. 150 men from Batt" in Coy. (11th N.F.).	J.C.
do	3rd		Extra working party 100 men. 9" Yorks for work on deep "trenches other parties as above. Lectures 11th N.F. on dug-outs.	J.C.
do	4th		Still raining. 11th N.F. relieved by 13th D.L.I. on Lorette Spur.	
do	5th		Rain. 2 Sections 1st Field Coy. R.M. Div. Engr.s were attached to me & reported for duty. Working party too much [?]	
do	6th		Started work on Central Bazyan in addition.	
do	7th		Rain. Work as above. Working parties 800 men.	J.C.
do	8th		— do — 700 men. 2 'C' Coy. 9.G.R. & Lewis 9" S.Staff attached to me for duty.	
do	9th		— do — — do — 13th D.L.I. relieved by 8" Yorks (Major Hawks). Wet. Work as above. Started Batt" platoons on dug out work 5 dug outs for M.G. Dets and 3 deep dug outs in hand. Work progressing at an average rate of 4 to 5 inches an hour. RE sections, 9" S.Staff and 'A' Coy. 11th Rot. Batt" at work.	
do	10th		Rained all day. No working parties. N°4 section marched to THIEPVAL 15 miles. One section 1/3 London 7.0.P.M. Left 10 p.m.	J.C.
do	11th		— do — arrived to take over Lorette Spur.	
do	12th		Packing up for move. Maj. Birch & Remainder L/3 London Field Co. R.E. arrived. All work inspected & handed over. Scout maps, documents, lists of dug-outs etc. handed over & receipts taken. Rained all day & all night. Company marched out from camp 8.45 p.m.	
LA THIEPLOYE	13th		Arrived 1.53 a.m. Got into billets and rested. Dull cold rainy. Everyone wet through. R.E draft 9 rank & file.	J.C.
do	14th		Cloudy. Cold rain at intervals. Smoke helmet + P.H. clothing inspection etc. Machine inspection in platoons.	J.C.
do	15th		Rained First Cl. marched off again via VALHUON, PETIT-ANVIN to VERCHIN. 16 mile march. Arrived 2.15 p.m. Held up ½ an hour by 35th Div" at VALHUON	J.C.
VERCHIN	16th		June marched to MATTRINGHEM via LUGY. Left 10 a.m. arrived 11.30 a.m. About 5 miles. Got into billets.	J.C.

2353 Wt. W2544/1454 700,000 5/15 D. D. & L. A.D.S.S./Forms/C. 2118.

WAR DIARY / INTELLIGENCE SUMMARY

Army Form C. 2118.

101st Field Co. R.E.
June 1916.

Place	Date	Hour	Summary of Events and Information	Remarks and references to Appendices
MATTRINGHEM	17th June 1916.	—	Practising bridging with trestles, loading & unloading pontoon wagons.	H/C
"	18th	—	Church parade in field 9.0am. Trestle bridging in afternoon.	
"	19th	—	Practising drill for pontoon bridges and making trestle bridges.	
"	20th	—	Practising company in extended order drill, attack, lecture on R.E. duties in the attack and demonstration of wire, wire cutting, wire entanglements, etc. Bend pt. picket. Sgt. 2 n.c.o.s 3 days. (3 O'clock patrol.) 2 N.C.O.s out away working all wagons, pontoons & trestles. 2 N.C.O.s away fatigues. Musketry & Bayonet practice, Newton Bros. doing section drill.	
"	21st	—	Co. on extended order drill, musketry and bayonet exercises.	H/C
"	22nd	—	Sgt. Peake (munition worker) appointed 2nd Lt. today. Sgt. Brown sent home as munition worker instead. Sapper Hurst L/Cpl (paid) yesterday, and Sapper Haynes appointed L/Cpl today. L/Cpl Henderson fell off his horse and hurt himself. In field today. Lt. Ambulance	J/C
do	23rd	—	C.R.E. inspected company officers and drill. Fatigues bathing parade. R. Henderson R.E. sent to Lt. Ambulance.	
do	24th	—	Still raining. Company marched to LILLERS in two parties. 1st Party consisting of all the company wagons except pontoon & trestle wagons & loading party under Lt. Baird. R.E. March 17 miles. 1st Party 1.30pm all ranks 62 horses. 3 four wheeled vehicles 19 wagons. 2 tons baggage. 2nd Party 6.30pm 23 all ranks 19 horses. 3 four wheeled vehicles 8 tons baggage. 1st Party entrained at LILLERS at 11.50pm.	H/C
YZEUX	25th	—	2nd Party entrained at LILLERS at 5.50am. 1st Party arrived at LONGUEAU at 8am, marched to YZEUX. Took halts on the way for breakfast and tea. arrived YZEUX at 5.30pm. 2nd Party arrived at YZEUX at 8.30pm. March about 15 miles. Men rather tired & footsore.	H/C
YZEUX	26th	—	Fixing up billets. Kit-inspections, bathing parades, drill etc. French Interpreter MOTTET reported for duty.	H/C
do	27th	—	Bayonet drill. batting parades etc.	
do	28th	—	Packing up wagons etc. Co. marched to ALLONVILLE via LA CHAUSSEÉ, LONGPRÉ, AMIENS. Distance 15 miles. Billeting party 1 NCO. and 6 men under Lt. Brown R.E. and French Interpreter. Starting point cross roads ACCEUIL at 7.30am. A' parade 2.30pm. Road orders three C.R.E. to standfast. Time 12.30 pm.	H/C
do	29th	—	C.E standing fast. C.E. I Corps Genl. Jolly inspected wet drill.	
do	30th	—	Reveille 4am. Horses & wagons ? Co. marched off at 12 noon. to ALLONVILLE route as above. 2 hours halt at Longpré for ? Arrived in billets 8.30pm. 16 mile march.	J/C Coutier R.E. O.C. 101 Coy R.E.

23/ July

101. F.RE
Vol 12

War Diary
of
101st Field Company, R.E.

from 1st July 1916 to 31st July 1916

(Volume 11)

Secret

WAR DIARY
INTELLIGENCE SUMMARY.
(Erase heading not required.)

Army Form C. 2118.

101st Field Co. R.E.

July 1916.

Instructions regarding War Diaries and Intelligence Summaries are contained in F. S. Regs., Part II. and the Staff Manual respectively. Title pages will be prepared in manuscript.

Place	Date	Hour	Summary of Events and Information	Remarks and references to Appendices
Allonville	1st July 1916		Kit inspection, clean arms inspection, foot inspection etc. Lieut Podmore off duty with bad knee today. Received 2 reinforcements today. Five Water for horses from L'Hallue River. Qu VERRIER. The ponds in the village are very foul and horses won't drink the water. Company to be ready to move at 6 hours notice from 12 noon today. All greatcoats dumped.	
La Houssoye	2nd		Company left for LA HOUSSOYE at 9.30pm Standing fast ready to move to BAISIEUX.	DA
Mellincourt	3rd		Got orders to go to MELLINCOURT where we bivouaced for the night. Moved to BELLUE FARM (East of ALBERT) Horses and transport remained in ALBERT. No orders for work came, no company went back to billets — ALBERT.	DA
ALBERT	4th		Company (Gaetino & 2 sections FHA) went to BECOURT WOOD at 7pm and waited for instructions to work. Company not required so went back to ALBERT arriving there at 11.45pm.	DA
do	5th		Company engaged in enemy wire cut up to SCOTS REDOUBT and returned to billets. MAJOR I.J CONNOR killed by a shell at about 6pm antetreated at ROUND WOOD (X.21.d) and buried by 53rd Field Ambulance in Cemetery just south of FRICOURT.	DA
do	6th		Standing fast in billets.	DA
do	7th		Paraded for work at CONTALMAISON at 2.45pm and marched to rendezvous near BECOURT (F.2.c.0.0.) Moved to 24 Bde H.Q. (F.2.b.9.9) at and got orders to report to O.C. 1st Worcester Regt at X.27.b.2.5. No work for us. Returned	DA

WAR DIARY
INTELLIGENCE SUMMARY

101st Field Co. R.E.
July 1916.
Army Form C. 2118.

Place	Date	Hour	Summary of Events and Information	Remarks and references to Appendices
ALBERT	7th		to Bdge. H.Q. and bivouaced for night. 1 O.R. wounded.	DI
do	8th		Standing by for work. Bivouaced for night without ranking. 2 O.R. wounded	DI
do	9th		Returned to billets at ALBERT.	DI
do	10th		Paraded for work at 12.45pm. Scots Redout. Left for CONTALMAISON at 7pm and were heavily shelled in communication trench and open ground just south of CONTALMAISON. Returned to bivouac at F2c 00. Bivouacs 1 O.R. Killed 3 O.R. Wounded.	DI
do	11th		Left at 11am. for CONTALMAISON and made strong point round crossroads at X16 d H. About 5 hours work done. Returned to billets ALBERT at about 8pm.	DI
do	12th		Company went out to billets at FRANVILLERS	DI
FRANVILLERS	13th		Inspection of equipment and clothing etc. of company. Moved off at 3.45p to MOLLIENS au BOIS.	DI DI
MOLLIENS au BOIS	14th		Capt R. A. TURNER R.E. arrived this morning and took up duty as O.C. Coy. Men crowded in billets which are not too good. Horse lines good. III Corps want us to make fascines in wood B8+9. Three section go to cut brushwood, but promised lorry with tools did not turn up till evening.	RE
	15th		Parade 6.30 am. 1, 2 + 4 Sections go out to work with fascines returns. Task allotted 100 fascines. No 3 works on billets.	RE

2333 Wt. W2544/1454 700,000 5/15 D. D. & L.   A.D.S.S./Forms/C. 2118.

WAR DIARY

INTELLIGENCE SUMMARY

Army Form C. 2118.

101st (Fd) Company
July 16

Place	Date	Hour	Summary of Events and Information	Remarks and references to Appendices
MOLIENS AU BOIS	16		Sunday. Fascines 60 for 2.3 + 4. Company paid after lunch and passes granted to AMIENS (11) Voluntary service at 6pm. 19 all ranks. DADMS delighted with our Cant. Capt Br. Baird promoted to Captain as list from Oct 4. 15. Fascines 100 for 1.3 + 4. Passes again for AMIENS.	
	17		Do.	
	18			
	19		Made 120 fascines each day.	
	20			
	21		Marched at 9am at tail of 69th Inf Brigade (None of our men fell out) and arrived in bivouacs just East of MAILLY MILLENCOURT at 2pm. Our field was walled with manure left by untidy predecessors. Weather was favourable.	
MILLENCOURT	22		Rifle Inspection at 9am. Drill (Oms) 2.30pm. Ready to move at ½ hours notice after dark. Go to sleep to the sound of a terrific bombardment.	
	23		Sunday. Parade 9am. Services for R.C. + N.C. 2.30pm. Backwards to company by 2 Br Buckm on gas etc. We are now continuing the training.	
	24		9am Physical drill 10.15am bayonet training 12 noon Offr Band & RE lecture on first aid. Starling arrives for Sappers Prisoners.	
	25		No 1 Section leave for BECOURT WOOD at 2pm. Arrived at 4.30pm & bivouaced. Sapper MACKIE awarded Military Medal	

Army Form C. 2118.

10/2t Field Company R.E.
July 1916

WAR DIARY
or
INTELLIGENCE SUMMARY.
(Erase heading not required.)

Place	Date	Hour	Summary of Events and Information	Remarks and references to Appendices
MILLENCOURT	26		Nos 2, 3 and 4 sections march to BECOURT WOOD taking section carts and water cart. H Q company in ALBERT (W29c25) I/C Capt Baird R.E. Horses lines on AMIENS Road (E3c55)	
ALBERT	27		No 3 section remains at BECOURT WOOD, remainder of company moves to trenches near SHELTER WOOD at X23c07 Sections cut's at SHELTER WOOD. Nos 1 and 2 sections making new Brigade H.Q. at VILLA WOOD (X12c57). No 4 section on night work digging new front trench at S.2.C. Three portion wagon loads of material taken to MIDDLE WOOD (X12c54) thus starting our company Dump. St Podumn was his way in no mans land and started to lay a shell hole to Bois trench.	R.E.
nr SHELTER WOOD	28.		1.+2. Coys at Villa wood 9am — 3p. two reliefs of 3 to follow thro' the night work finishing last night work, strong post + wire in front. No 1. section return to B.W. 2nd Lt. W. Owen wounded.	R.E.
	29		BECOURT returned by no 3. 2.+3. work at Villa wood. no 4. wiring again 2off. + 6 o.r. wounded - one died of Gd. Davis.	R.E.
	30.		2+3 Villa Wood. 1 relief of 3.	R.E.
	31		2+3 Villa Wood. No 1. undertakes Medical Aid Dugout deep shaft in front 23.	

C.H.R.E.
O.C. 10/1st Fd Co R.E.

23rd Divisional Engineers

101st FIELD COMPANY R. E.

AUGUST 1 9 1 6

Vol 13

War Diary
of
101st Field Company, Royal Engineers
from 1st August 1916 to 31st August 1916.
(Volume 12)

WAR DIARY or INTELLIGENCE SUMMARY

Army Form C. 2118.

AUGUST 1916

10 (Fd) Coy R.E.

Place	Date	Hour	Summary of Events and Information	Remarks and references to Appendices
Stirwood	1		Villa Wood. Dug out nos 2 & 3. Lt Shaw sees in/fabric in front line to organize system. Each company is to provide 50 men for a 4 hour task as by R.E. on their own work. Supper & O/H Walker arrives at Bécourt, a mile from No 4. relieves no 125.	
do	2		Villa Wood. nos 4 & 3. Lt Shaw continues his front line dugout and organizing of work. A lot of men are get to light duty.	
"	3		Villa Wood. nos 4 & 3. No 1. front line. No 2 relieves no 3. Gas lessons in evening. Reluct. effective.	
"	4		do do. nos 2 & 4, do	
"	5		do do. nos 2 & 4. No 1. front line dragons. Sickness in redwood. from 4am	
"	6		No 2 working in sap S2C.75 worked till 2am. mostly in full view of Boche. Lt Ginham was so close that he was able to distinguish Loch of "Kultur" in their features. He would have worked all day and probably got on well with the work, but our heavies decided to have a shoot. In the night Lt Hutchit continued relaying and got to the road. It has been hoped he would get through later. He got back to camp at 9.30am. after a good nights work. Lt. Rodham arranged details of attack in morning of 7th with O.C. Battalion N.F.	
"	7		No 4 went to assemble in sap at about 5.30 am. Surprise attack by the 25 Infantry turned out to be no surprise at all. 15 could not leave the trench, the R.E. and Infantry were went with drawn after blowing up 30' from road. These afmathians were about by the 75 Fd Coy. 15 Div. at of 3pm. marched to FRANVILLERS.	

WAR DIARY or INTELLIGENCE SUMMARY.

Army Form C. 2118.

10th Field Coy R.E.

August 1916

Place	Date	Hour	Summary of Events and Information	Remarks and references to Appendices
FRANVILLERS	6	—	Cleaning billets. Inspection of clothing & equipment.	DM
	9	—	Cleaning wagons all morning. Too hot to do much in afternoon. Company marched chits etc. 2=6pl. ATCHERLEY M.C. 4 2= Cpl HURST J. to be acting corporals. Sapper CANNON J. & Pioneer HANSEN M. to paid Lancecorporals at Podume & 2.0 R leave MERICOURT at 4 p.m. to proceed by rail to BAILLEUL. No advance party.	DM
MUZE	10		Mounted section paraded 12.30 p.m. & marched to CORDONETTE and billeted. Lt. Bircham and 2 sappers with bicycles entrained MERICOURT 5.15 p.m. for LONGPRÉ to arrange billets	RS
COQUEREL	11		Mounted section marched at 4.30 am reached COQUEREL on the SOMME 2 p.m. and billeted. Sappers under Lt. Shaw marched to FRECHENCOURT & entrained for LONGPRÉ marched to COQUEREL arriving 6 p.m.	RS
	12		Billeted in SOMME	RS
	13		Company marched to LONGPRÉ & entrained 3.30 p.m. for BAILEUL	RS
	14		arrived BAILLEUL 12.30 am (only 9 hours in train) marched to billets 1 mile N of METEREN.	RS
METEREN	15.		Rested. O.C. Bn. Shaw & Lineker & 2 N.C.O's proceeded to PLOEGSTEERT to take over from 2.2.5 Fd Coy. R.E. A surprising lot, many of trenches and a lot of work done.	RS
E PLOEGSTEERT	16		Company marched at 9 am to PLOEGSTEERT and took over. Horse lines also good.	RS

Army Form C. 2118.

WAR DIARY
or
INTELLIGENCE SUMMARY.   101st Fd Coy RE

(Erase heading not required.)

Instructions regarding War Diaries and Intelligence
Summaries are contained in F. S. Regs., Part II.
and the Staff Manual respectively. Title pages
will be prepared in manuscript.

AUGUST.

Place	Date	Hour	Summary of Events and Information	Remarks and references to Appendices
PUEGSTEERT	17th		Company handed 7 am. for work. Two section 2+4 on left & 3+1 on right no infantry parties arranged yet. C.R.E. visited coy and explained system of getting working parties.	RE
	18th	7.30 am	parade for work. Infantry arrange.	
	19th		ditto	
			See 200 if more than we want.	
	20th		ditto	
			Night nos. 2+4 small parties about 3+0x of fort trench as no means have ready for jump, wire later for pieces laid 4.0x in advance.	
	21st		10 W.R.R. 350 party dig to ault under R.E. 60 pieces of S.S. Coffs. put up the wire. A success fine night. Sutton had holiday.	
	22nd		Coy attruck to 5 Fd Arty, Capt Bauer took infantry (200).	
	23rd		Work as usual. Sgt Wing had dismissed after 4 days trenches	
	24th		Returned. Brighter weather. O.R.E. went round section	
	25th		Brigade with Sutton worked afternoon.	
	26th		Work as usual. 2nd Lt Askew arrived from 125 Fd Coy	
	27th		Work as usual. Digging lines for 70th I.B. slight night parties did not turn up.	
	28th		Lt Pedmore left to join 125 Fd Coy, work as usual.	
	29th		Work as usual	
	30th			
	31st		Work delayed owing to heavy rain. Work is defence with wit trenches. Parties nearly as usual & gas.	

Vol 14

23

War Diary
of
101st Field Company, Royal Engineers

from 1st September 1916. to 30th September 1916.

(Volume 13)

WAR DIARY or INTELLIGENCE SUMMARY

101st Field Co. R.E. Army Form C. 2118.

SEPTEMBER 1916

Place	Date	Hour	Summary of Events and Information	Remarks and references to Appendices
PLOEGSTEERT	1		Work as usual	DM
	2		Company resting. Received orders to move by MOON on 3rd. Guns slewn at 11 hrs. Above carried out at 11.50 p.m.	DM
	3		Mounted section moved off at 9 am & dismounted portion at 11 am leaving eighteen miles and a quiet part of the line kept Tunnel, 2nd Lt Lindsay & Hurkstep remained behind and shewed half relieving company (51st) new section in afternoon, & reported up new billet at night.	DM
La Bousse near BAILLEUL	4		Company resting. Cleaning wagons. Subunit to be bought for company.	DM
	5		2nd Lt Hurkstep left with party to billet in TILQUES area. 2nd Lt active left at 9 am to billet for mounted section of 3 Company at HONDEGHEM. Capt Baird & three subaltern transport left at 10 am. arrived HONDEGHEM at 2 p.m. Dismounted portion of company left at 12.45 arrived at BAILLEUL Station entrained & detrained at ST OMER after a much delayed journey (23 hrs late) marched to BLEUE MAISON (WATTEN) and arrived after dark.	DM
BLEUE MAISON (WATTEN)	6		Company resting. Mounted section left HONDEGHEM at 8 am and marched to BLEUE MAISON via ST OMER arrived 4 p.m. at dinner.	DM
	7		Cleaning billets and all wagons.	DM
	8		Communication drill. Section & squad drill.	DM

Army Form C. 2118.

WAR DIARY
INTELLIGENCE SUMMARY.
(Erase heading not required.)

10th Field Coy R.E.   SEPTEMBER 1916.

Place	Date	Hour	Summary of Events and Information	Remarks and references to Appendices
BLEUE MAISON	9th		Morning, section + company drill. Afternoon, sports. Enemy aircraft.	D/
	10th		Company left at 9am and marched to ARQUES Station & entrained. Entraining finished at 1.45pm. Train departed at 2.39pm. Arrived SALEUX (Amiens) at 11.15pm detrained and marched to ALLONVILLE arriving there at 4.30am on 11th. Village very crowded	D/ D/
ALLONVILLE	11th		Afternoon clerk parade.	Billets
	12th		Paraded 9am and marched to BRESTLE arriving at 2pm. Very scant but good water supply.	D/
BRESTLE	13th		Rifle inspection etc.	
	14th		Cleaning wagons + equipment	
	15th		Cleaning wagons + erecting 4 hut shelters. Scheme with 69 & 70 Inf Bde. Finishing erection of huts. Company ready to move off on 2hrs notice.	
	16		Constructing deep pit latrines at five parts of the village. Making new pattern fly-proof front seats. Suffers doing bayonet drill. Driver	D/
	17		Marching order parade (mounted) & riding drill. L./Cpt Lunnen to 10am work no preceding day.	D/
	18		Work on latrines. 2nd Lt Kinsland to Hospital Sick.	D/
	19		Paraded 8am and marched to BECOURT WOOD and took over very few billets from 91st Field Co RE. Afternoon took over work from 74 Field Co RE. Horse lines at DERNANCOURT.	D/
BECOURT WOOD	20		Working on CONTALMAISON–LABOISSELLE and CONTALMAISON–MARTINPUICH roads. Shift of horse lines to BECOURT WOOD.	D/

101st Field Co. R.E. Army Form C. 2118.

WAR DIARY
or
INTELLIGENCE SUMMARY. — SEPTEMBER 1916.
(Erase heading not required.)

Instructions regarding War Diaries and Intelligence Summaries are contained in F. S. Regs., Part II, and the Staff Manual respectively. Title pages will be prepared in manuscript.

Place	Date	Hour	Summary of Events and Information	Remarks and references to Appendices
BECOURT	21		Work on roads as usual. 400 working party	DD
WOOD	22		Work on roads as usual. Carpenters renew in camp working fly proof meat safes, latrines & grease traps. 1 O.R. wounded, 10.R. wounded, at duty. S. Stella fell in road at 7.30 p.m. and later & at 9.30 p.m. No casualties here. 400 working party as usual.	DD
	23		Work on roads as usual. 400 working party. Working camp as usual.	DD
	24		do do do	DD
		6.00	do	DD
	25	5.30	1st Parade. 400 working party	DD
	26		Work as usual. 1 O.R. wounded. 460 working party at 10.30 p.m. 5.O.R. wounded. Hostile aircraft dropped 10 bombs in wood. 1 mule hit anm. present	DD
	27		Work as usual. 5 reinforcements arrived. 400 working party	DD
	28		Work as usual. No working party	DD
	29		Work as usual.	DD
	30		Work as usual. 5 O.R. wounded	DD

Bland Captain for
O.C. 101st Field Co. R.E.

Vol 15

War Diary
of
101st Field Company
Royal Engineers
October 1st to October 31st, 1916
(Volume 14)

101st Field Coy R.E.   Army Form C. 2118.

WAR DIARY
or
INTELLIGENCE SUMMARY.   OCTOBER 1916

(Erase heading not required.)

Place	Date	Hour	Summary of Events and Information	Remarks and references to Appendices
BECOURT WOOD	1		Working ordary and turning point on Road LA BOISSELLE – CONTALMAISON. Working party 100 inf. Loying fascines on CONTALMAISON – MARTIN PUICH Road at X.6.c.72. and laying rubble. Fine weather. Latter job frequently shelled with 4.2's.	DJ.
	2		Work as yesterday. Very wet day.	DJ.
	3		Work as yesterday. Ditching completed. Pit props being used in MARTINPUICH Road job as outfit of fascines have run out. Drift may give in below.	DJ.
	4		Work same as yesterday. Still wet weather.	DJ.
	5		Work as usual. (No infantry.)	DJ.
	6		Work as usual.	DJ.
	7		Work as usual.	DJ.
	8		Work as usual. 2 men 100 inf. working party. 2 men go on leave.	DJ.
	9		Company left BECOURT WOOD at 9 am and marched to BRESTLE and bivouacked. All maps etc handed over to 74th Field Co. 15th Division. Company cadre for no. ???.	DJ.
BRESTLE	10		Gun parade. Inspection of rifles. Cleaning wagons.	DJ.
	11		Mounted portion of company marched away at 10 a.m. formed part of 70th Bde. transport. Watered feed at PONT NOYELLES. This took 2½ hours. Billeted at St. SAVEUR at 7 pm & found their billetting officer had disappeared. Bivouacked on horse lines.	STJ.
ST SAVEUR	12		Mounted section left at 6.30 am and marched to COCQUEREL arriving at 12 noon. Sappers left BRESTLE at 10 am to entrain at ALBERT. Entrained at 4 pm. and	DJ.
COCQUEREL	13		Arrived at COCQUEREL at LONGPRE Station at 7 am! marched to COCQUEREL arriving at 9.15 am. Company resting. Billet & weather good. 2 Lt. W. ALLEN R.E. joined.	DJ.

161st Field Co. R.E. Army Form C. 2118.

WAR DIARY
or
INTELLIGENCE SUMMARY
(Erase heading not required.)

OCTOBER 1916

Place	Date	Hour	Summary of Events and Information	Remarks and references to Appendices
COCQUEREL	14	—	Paraded 9.30am and marched to MILLENCOURT (just North of ABBEVILLE) arriving about 1 p.m. and stayed the night in good billets	D.I.
MILLENCOURT	15		Paraded mounted section at 9am & Sappers at 10am and marched to CONTEVILLE Station & entrained complete. Train departed at 3.30hrs. and arrived at HOUPOUTRE siding POPERINGHE at 9pm. Marched to HALIFAX Camp H14 c 3.5 arrived at	
HALIFAX CAMP	16		12.30 a.m. This camp is near VLAMERTINGHE. 6.30am parade. Cleaning huts and waggons.	
	17		Cleaning billets & waggons. Paraded 6.30p. and marched to billets in cellars at YPRES. Horse lines remain at H14.	
YPRES	18		Setting into billets	
	19		Work started in left brigade sector. Our front is divided into Sections, this front line @ (1) LEINSTER ST. (2) BOND ST. (3) LOVERS WALK @ front line work also billets undertaken over from 47 Field Coy. Australian Engineers.	
	20		Work as usual	
	21		do	
	22		do	
	23		Company voting	
	24		Work as usual	
	25		do	
	26		do	
	27		do	
	28		do	
	29			
	30		Battd Gen to be Adjs Work as usual	
	31		Work as usual	

R. Winter
O.C. 161 Co. R.E.

Vol 16

War Diary
of
101st Field Company
Royal Engineers.

From 1st November 1916 – 30th November 1916.

(Volume 5)

Registered

Army Form C. 2118.

WAR DIARY
or
INTELLIGENCE SUMMARY. 101 Fd Coy RE
(Erase heading not required.)   November

Instructions regarding War Diaries and Intelligence
Summaries are contained in F. S. Regs., Part II.
and the Staff Manual respectively. Title pages
will be prepared in manuscript.

Place	Date	Hour	Summary of Events and Information	Remarks and references to Appendices
YPRES.	1st		Work as usual. Gas instructions on Kratzer & Oxford St. No.2 section on LOVERS WALK	
	2nd 3rd		No 3 WARRINGTON AVENUE between Town Walls & H.Q. Reserve at the extension	
	4th		No 4 on Bastion of Earl St. R.A. dugouts & shelters for Gurkhas M.G.	
	5 6		work as above next day	
	6 Oir		Commenced work on above	
	[illegible]		worked on above dut H.Q. dugouts started at Halfway House	
	10 11		St Shews retired from line. Not dug.	
	12		work on above. from Hullugh R.A. dugout started on new extension.	
	13 14		work as above next day	
	17		acid fast started for ADMS at Halfway House	
	18 19		work as above	
	20		19 on arms. Works on Church Wall started, Capt Basso gone on leave	
	21		work on above	
	22		10 on arms. Not delay.	

2353 Wt. W2544/1454 700,000 5/15 D. D. & L. A.D.S.S./Forms/C. 2118.

Army Form C. 2118.

WAR DIARY
or
INTELLIGENCE SUMMARY. 4th FT CORPS November (cont)
(Erase heading not required.)

Place	Date	Hour	Summary of Events and Information	Remarks and references to Appendices
YPRES	23		Saffron Steam killed on Warrington Avenue, work as above.	
	24		Work commenced at junction of LEINSTER ST. work as above	
	25			
	26		Geneva Serum Wall in trestles except for a few given details	
	27		Roselyn St trestles finished not being	
	28		work as above	
	29			
	30		5.00 joined the company, work as above	

3.12.16

R. Sim
Capt RE
O.C. in RE CoyRE

Vol 17

War Diary
of
101st Field Coy R.E.
from 1st December to 31st December 1916.

(Volume No. 16)

Secret

WAR DIARY
or
INTELLIGENCE SUMMARY.

1/5th L'pool RR
DECEMBER 1916.

Army Form C. 2118.

(Erase heading not required.)

Place	Date	Hour	Summary of Events and Information	Remarks and references to Appendices
YPRES	1st		Foggy day. Batn. worked as usual. Shower baths on entrails at gunners dugout by railway. Program as here shown.	
	2nd		St Michaels Clergymen the Coburg GRR out and less. Stated youth on Menin = Bapre Road Ypres streets.	
	3rd/1		Opt-Bacot was to trench company	
	4th		Rest day	
	5th		O.C. went on leave. Work as usual	
	6th		Work as usual	
	6½		Everything with Left now in dugouts below Lost street started	
	7th		Work as usual	
	8th		Ringfence concrete part for M.G. dugout given House started	
	9th		2nd Portsmouth R.E. held at Zillebeke. Rest day.	
	10th		Coy/uty M.Q. Hill 60 completed.	
	11th		Work as usual	
	12th		do	
	13th		do	
	14th		do	
	14½		Rest Day. Took over left Battalion, Right Brigade front	
	15th		Egypt. Now Extend Mechanicton started	
	16th		Started Company H.Q. Wellington Crescent	
	17th		Gas post at Half pipe / Ypres started	
	18½			
	19th			

WAR DIARY
INTELLIGENCE SUMMARY

101st Field Company RE
DECEMBER 1916

Place	Date	Hour	Summary of Events and Information	Remarks and references to Appendices
YPRES	20th		Work as usual.	
	21st		Daywork on Kemmel St stopped by shelling. O O returns from leave.	
			Reconnoitred trench at CRAB CRAWL.	
	22nd		Ran line of cond. for new trench. Night works fatn. duties no show as usual.	
	23rd		Resting.	
	24th		Put in trench at BIRR X ROADS. Tried trench at CRAB CRAWL	
	25th		Put [?] at 1am. but could not be worked.	
	26th		Started work on 4 Mrs outlier tunnels. Two — RITZ ST & 2 in WELLINGTON CRESCENT.	
	27th		Arranging to lay new track. Ret Ravine dugouts. Trains not arranged so show cancelled.	
	28th		Trench dugs. live adits. Bad weather from results average 2ft deep x 2ft wide	
	29th		Started 9 cupola dugouts in MAPLE ST with no success. Withdrawn for later work.	
	30th		Oxford Street. Clearing (two bays out & taken away)	
	31st		Tunnels in mg emplacements seem a failure, asked CRE for advice (still to wait)	
			Pumps at BIRR X ROADS still not working.	

[signature]
R.A. [?] RE
Major RE
O.C. 101 F.C.R.E.

1.1.17

Vol 18

Volume 19

War Diary

of

101st Field Company R.E.

From
January 1st 1917
to
January 31st 1917

Secret

Army Form C. 2118.

WAR DIARY
or
INTELLIGENCE SUMMARY.
(Erase heading not required.)

10. Fd Coy RE

January 1917

Place	Date	Hour	Summary of Events and Information	Remarks and references to Appendices
YPRES	1st 1917		St Michels proceeds on leave. Advice on tunnels, hotbeds. Dump service to Pay No 2 batteries night working parts. Shaft for Battalion HQ. OXFORD ST. Started.	
	2nd		Supm Belloch, RE Tunnelling Coy inspects all mining dugouts. Loads 12 cubort mines tested. Prepared ready for use	
	3rd		Red Lamp Gordon House sleeves repaired	
	4th		2nd mine lent to Colonel repaired. Motor Pumps at Bus & Rlo repaired & refilled	
	5th		Fort Rlect Refugies finished	
	6th		Repairs to dugs at regina	
	7th		Dam in Culv 30 - Bits & Rlo trestflooring	
	8th		Dam on aq- Bits & Rlo trestflooring 9 Coy H.Q.	
	9th		YPRES heavily shelled footbridge at Lilly Post blown in air. two places. Repairs temporarily. 9 Coys Cookhouse sheltered.	
	10th		LEINSTER ST blown in. Drain cut across MENIN RD to drain water from am in FOREST. ST.	
	11th		55 Bus staff. O.C. forwarded in Circuit instructions to R.P. regn Road repairs on M.R. up to WELLINGTON CRESCENT	
	12th		M.G. Emp. armt in.	
	13th		Roof of S.A.P at Batt HQ. OXFORD ST feet in. NK1 Hacksap removed from leave	
	14th		Work as usual	
	15th		2nd Batt front Right Engrs. handed over to 128th Field Coy	
	16th		H.G 60 bombarded	
	17th			
	18th		11. P. Allen proceeded on leave.	
	19th		O.C returns from leave. O/c in his absence	
	20th		Lt. Clarke evacuated to C.C.S.	
	21st			
	22nd		Work as usual	
	23rd			

101st Field Coy. R.E.   Army Form C. 2118.

WAR DIARY
or
INTELLIGENCE SUMMARY.

January 1917

Place	Date	Hour	Summary of Events and Information	Remarks and references to Appendices
YPRES	24th		Rest day. Frost	
	25th		Entrance to system of dugouts at Half Way House started	
	26th		Concreting stopped at Gordon House dugout owing to frost.	
	27th		Work as usual. Frost	
	28th		"	
	29th		Cylinders of picric acid engine at BIRR X-RDS sent to be repaired.	
	30th		"Faees in" Cdr. RITZ ST. tunnel	
	31st		Welton 2½ H.P. pump installed at BIRR X-RDS installing	

J.A. Munro RE
Major
O.C. 101st Fd Coy RE

2.2.17

Vol 19

War Diary
of
101st Field Coy RE.

from 1st February 1917 to 28th February 1917.

(Volume 18)

Army Form C. 2118.

101st Field Company R.E.

FEBRUARY 1917

WAR DIARY
or
INTELLIGENCE SUMMARY.
(Erase heading not required.)

Instructions regarding War Diaries and Intelligence Summaries are contained in F. S. Regs., Part II. and the Staff Manual respectively. Title pages will be prepared in manuscript.

Place	Date	Hour	Summary of Events and Information	Remarks and references to Appendices
YPRES S	1st		Rest day. Bnd. continued	
	2nd		North tunnel in WELLINGTON CRESCENT recommenced	
	3rd		Work as usual	
	4th		do	
	5th			
	6th		Sandbagging in truce St practically stopped owing to frozen ground. Work as usual	
	7th		LEINSTER ST ground up sunk front line.	
	8th		Deepening COTTAGE ST started	
	9th		Rest day.	
	10th		Revetting of WEST ST started	
	11th		LEINSTER als OXFORD STREETS should hurry.	
	12th		Than ratos in. GORDON Hº M.G. emplacement recommenced.	
	13th		Work as usual	
	14th		do	
	15th			
	16th		Bus track do. from Halfway House to Oxford St started.	
	17th		Rest day	
	18th		Tunnel at BIRR X-RDS through to North side of MENIN RD.	
	19th		Work as usual	
	20th		do	
	21st		Lt Fri[?]/King reports for duty.	
	22nd		MAPLE FORT M.G. Emplacement finished.	
	23rd		Work as usual	
	24th		do	
	25th		Rest day.	
BUSSEBOOM	26th		Company move to BUSSEBOOM. Lt Russel reports for duty.	
	27th		" " HERZEELE	
	28th			

Major R.E.
O.C. 101st Field Company R.E.

Vol 2.

War Diary

of

101st Field Company R.E.

from

March 1st 1917

to

March 31st 1917

Volume 19.

WAR DIARY 161st Field Company R.E.
INTELLIGENCE SUMMARY. MARCH 1917.

Army Form C. 2118.

Place	Date	Hour	Summary of Events and Information	Remarks and references to Appendices
HERZEELE	1st		Company move to BROXEELE	
BROXEELE	2nd		Fatigues in billets and stables. Cleaning wagons.	
"	3rd		Training	
"	4th		Rest day. No 1 section move to WORMHOUDT for work on Laundry	
"	5th & 10th		Lt Russell and 11 O.Rs evacuated to F.R.S., WORMHOUDT	
"	11th		Training	
"	12th		Rest day.	
"	13th		No 1 section rejoins Company. Training	
"	14th		Lt Russell rejoins company. "	
"	15th		Training	
"	16th		" Lt Arthur rejoins Company	
"	17th		" Cleaning and loading wagons.	
"	18th		"	
"	19th		Rest day.	
HERZEELE	20th		Move to HERZEELE area.	
HOUTKERQUE	21st		HOUTKERQUE area.	
"	22nd		Company fatigues.	
"	23rd		Training	
"	24th		"	
"	25th		Rest day.	
"	26th		C.R.E. Show motor lorries Routemant to STEENVORDE 10 mi.	
"	27th		No 3 and 4 Section move to VLAMERTINGHE for work on 2" line	
"	28th		The rest work bridges no 2 Scheme.	
"	29th		Inspection by Army Commander, good turn out, defaulters few	
"	30th		Training no 1 section scheme	
"	31st		Training Special attention to gas. Football vs signals won 3-0	
			Fat collection started.	

Capt R.E.
O.C. 161st Fd Coy RE

Vol 21

War Diary

of

101st Field Company R.E.

from

April 1st 1917

to

April 30th 1917.

Volume 20.

Army Form C. 2118.

WAR DIARY
or
INTELLIGENCE SUMMARY.
(Erase heading not required)

101st Coy RE
APRIL 1918

Instructions regarding War Diaries and Intelligence Summaries are contained in F.S. Regs., Part II. and the Staff Manual respectively. Title pages will be prepared in manuscript.

Place	Date	Hour	Summary of Events and Information	Remarks and references to Appendices
HOUTKERQUE	1st		Sections 1 & 2 training. Sections 3 & 4 repairs to "L" line.	
	2nd		Do.	
	3rd		Do.	
	4th		Do.	
	5th		Sections 3 & 4 rejoin company.	
	6th		Section 2 commence work on Divisional HQ, BUSSEBOOM	
FLAMERTINGHE H.13.d.5.3	7th		Company move to FLAMERTINGHE. Fatigues. Capt SHAW returns from leave.	
	8th		Rest day.	
	9th		Repairs to camp. Brick pathway round stables commenced.	
	10th		No 3 Section erect latrines at MONTREAL CAMP. No 4 Section make horse standings (for R.A.M.C. at BUSSEBOOM)	
	11th		" complete "	
	12th		No 1 Section start ammunition dump work as above. Harness inspection.	
	13th		YPRES to superintending work on new emplacements. B GRIFFIN and 7 NCOs move to RAMC stables finished	
	14th		Platform in Cinema WINNIPEG CAMP started Coal bunker at " "	
	15th		Rest day.	
	16th		Repair of splinter proof shelters at prisoners camp started (H.14 & 19) Cinema Platform finished	
	17th		" "	
	18th		Roadway at R.E. dumps H.17.c.7.3. started. O.C. goes on leave.	
	19th		Coal bunker finished.	
	20th		Bridges for R.A. at G.17.b.8.4. started	
	21st		Work as above.	
	22nd		Rest day. Box respirator drill.	
	23rd		Screen repairs at ammunition dump (H.14 c. & 9) completed. 6 Bridges for R.A. completed.	

WAR DIARY
or
INTELLIGENCE SUMMARY.

101st Field Co. R.E.

APRIL 1917. (Cont'd)

Army Form C. 2118.

Place	Date	Hour	Summary of Events and Information	Remarks and references to Appendices
VLAMERTINGHE H.13.d.5.8.	24.4.17		5 Bridges for R.A. started at H.8.d.3.8.	
	25.		2 Bridges for R.A. at G.17.b and G.17.a completed. Work as usual.	
	26			
	27		7 Bridges for R.A. completed at H.8.d. Obstacle course erected at TORONTO CAMP. Concealed hairpin dugout started at KRUITSTRAAT.	
	28.		Screen for new road to store started at H.22.b.3.9.	
	29		Rest day. Baths	
	30.		Work as usual.	

W.F. Shaw Capt. R.E.
for Major R.E.
Commanding
101st Field Co. R.E.

Vol 22

War Diary

of

101st Field Company R.E.

from

May 1st 1917

to

May 31st 1917.

Volume 21.

WAR DIARY or INTELLIGENCE SUMMARY

101st Field Company R.E.
MAY 1917
Army Form C. 2118.

Place	Date	Hour	Summary of Events and Information	Remarks and references to Appendices
VLAMERTINGHE	1st		Screens at H.14.b.5.8. and at H.22.b.39. completed.	
	2nd		Company move to STEENVOORDE.	
STEENVOORDE	3rd		Company inspected by G.O.C. 23rd Division.	
	4th		Route march.	
	5th		Company move to G.21.a.4.4. Brier Camp.	
G.21.a.4.4	6th		Work on HEKSKEN Ammunition dump started.	
	7th		do. do. continued	
	8th		do. do.	
	9th		do. do.	
	10th		Company moved to YPRES.	
YPRES	11th		Work started on ZILLEBEEKE DIVERSION, STEWART ST. and Saps F.G.H. RUM TRENCH and GAP TRENCH.	
	12th		New trench started from junction of OBSERVATORY TR. + REM TR. to junction of CANADA and LIVING TR.	
	13th		4 Officers and 100 Infantry attached for work. Lt. GRIFFIN and 12 R.E. attached to R.A. for work.	
	14th		1 Officer and 30 O.R. attached work on Infantry O.P's	
	15th		1 Section 128th R.E. with their attached Infantry from Company for work.	
	16th		New trench above named over to 5 STAFFORDS. 12 Ammunition dumps started at junction of MAPLE ST. and ZILLEBEEKE ST., 4 in CANADA ST. and 4 HEDGE ST.	
	17th		Clearing & Repairing DAVIDSON ST. ST PETERS ST. and FRONT LINE TRENCH I.30.d.8.79.	
	18th		Work as above.	
	19th		New trench started connecting ZILLEBEEKE ST. and VINCE ST. Repairs to ZILLEBEEKE ST. and WINNIPEG ST. started.	
	20th		Work as above.	

2353 Wt. W 2544/1454 700,000 5/15 D. D. & L. A.D.S.S./Forms/C. 2118.

WAR DIARY or INTELLIGENCE SUMMARY

Army Form C. 2118.

101st Field Coy R.E.

MAY 1917

Place	Date	Hour	Summary of Events and Information	Remarks and references to Appendices
YPRES	21st		Infantry O.Ps completed & working party of 1 officer and 20 O.R reporting to unit	
	22nd		Work as usual.	
	23rd		2 days Fatigue rations stored in YPRES	
	24th		Work as usual.	
	25th		Rest day	
	26th		1 Company 9th SOUTH STAFFORDS take on work in front trenches from Sap 'G' to LIVING TRENCH. (SANCTUARYWOOD sector)finishing work as usual. F.L. system keenly altered.	
	27th		Engineer Camp. at VALLEY COTTAGES, and battalion dumps at ARMAGH and Lt. RUSSELL rejoins Company.	
	28th			
	29th		K.F. GRIFFIN and 12 O.R attached to R.E.A. return to company	
	30th		Firestepping F.L. trench from [illegible] DEAD END to G's sap commenced	
	31st		Work as above.	

J.A. [illegible]
Major R.E.
Commanding 101st Coy R.E.

Vol 23

Confidential.

War Diary.

of

101st Field Company. R.E.

from

June 1st 1914

to

June 30th 1914

Volume 22.

WAR DIARY or INTELLIGENCE SUMMARY

Army Form C. 2118.

101st Field Company RE

JUNE 1917

Place	Date	Hour	Summary of Events and Information	Remarks and references to Appendices
YPRES	1st		Work in progress in following places - GAP ST., NEW TRENCH, ROUTE 'C', Assembly trenches behind F.L. from DEAD END & CANADA ST. and clearing blocks in F. Line and ST PETER'S ST and DAVIDSON ST.	
	2nd		Sappers and 25 O.R. from 6th Bde. Brigade are attached to Company for work.	
	3rd		Sappers from 128th O.R.J. join the Company. 2nd Australian 50 O.R. from 6th Brigade join the Company for work	
	4th			
	5th		Work as before. GAP ST and ZILLEBEEKE ST badly blown in.	
	6th		VALLEY COTTAGES DUMP shelled and not on fire (about 2 lorries destroyed). Repairs to ZILLEBEEKE ST. and GAP ST. RUM TR and OBSERVATORY TR. Company work to RITZ ST.	
	7th		2nd ARMY Offensive commenced. Strong points constructed at I.30.c.55,75 and I.30.a.7.6. Communication trench cut across NO MAN'S LAND from I.30.a.75,15 to I.30.a.7.0. Front line cleared and to IMAGE ROW to I.30.c.55.85. Support line started commencing at I.30.d.15.30 and running in a southerly direction to IMAGE AV.	
	8th		do.	
	9th		few support line continued.	
	10th/11th		do.	
	12th		Company move back to camp at H.13.d.34. Attached infantry rejoin their units.	
H.13.d.34	13th		19 Sappers at work in Div. R.E. Dump H.13.d.9.2. Erecting huts at MIC MAC CAMP at H.31.a.9.2.	
	14th		Hutting at MIC MAC CAMP	
	15th		Do	
BAILLEUL	16th		Company move to X.10.b.3.9. Shell 27. Erecting water troughs at H.33.d.9.2 and H.29.c.3.9
X.10.b.3.9	17th		Inspection by G.O.C. 23rd Division.	

WAR DIARY or INTELLIGENCE SUMMARY

Army Form C. 2118.

101st Field Company R.E. June 1917

Place	Date	Hour	Summary of Events and Information	Remarks and references to Appendices
X.10.c.3.9	18th June		Painting dugout Company fatigues	
	19th		do	
	20th		do	
	21st		do	
	22nd		do	
	23rd		Erecting attention bench, box latrines, incinerators and firing open.	
	24th		Painting wagons. Company fatigues. Preliminary show for R.E. turnouts. Divisional horse show.	
	25th		do	
	26th		As section drill.	
	27th June		Company Sports, Cinema.	
	28th		Company fatigues. R.O.C. Durin Capt SHAW R.E. came to take command of 228th 40 Gy R.	
	29th		Company moves to DICKEBUSCH. Desmal parade in decoration to the men	
DICKEBUSCH	30th		Company works on Light Railway running from VOORMEZEELE DUMP towards front line.	

R O Winter, R.E. C.L., R.E.
Major
O.C. 101 Fd Co R.E.

Appendix A.
    Casualties & Honours During tour in YPRES

May 12th 1917   Spr Elkins   Wounded.
    13th   Att. Infantry Officer   Killed
    14th   Spr. Truelove   Wounded (accidentally)
    21st   Spr Wright   }   Wounded
                   Spr Kent
    23rd   Cpl Shaw   }
                   Spr Watson   Wounded (at duty)
                   Spr Bryant
    24th   2 Cpl Pentzer   Wounded
    25th   Spr Sawyer T.   Wounded (at duty)
    26th   Spr Robins   Wounded (at Duty)
    28th   Spr Ray   }
                    " Rabbitts
                    " Allen   Wounded.
                    " Merry
                    " Foster
    29th   Pion. Hallard   Wounded.
June 4th 1917.   Spr. Hughes   Wounded
                   Spr. Laidlaw   awarded the MILITARY MEDAL.
     5th   C.S.M. Matthews   Wounded (at duty)
     7th   Sgt. Hurst   }
      "   "   Watson
      "   "   Cannon
                   Lce Cpl. Dawsley
                   Spr Burrell
                    " Fox   Wounded.
                    " Latimer
                    " Morgan
                    " Robinson
                    " Vosey
                   Pion. Johnston
                   2 Cpl. Pooly   }
                   Spr Plummer   Wounded (at duty)
                    " Grimwood

Appendix A.
Casualties & Honours during tour in YPRES.
(continued)

Date	Name	Status
June 7th 1917	Spr. Massey	Missing.
"	Pnr. Shipley	Killed.
8th	Pnr. Robinson	Killed.
"	Spr. White	Wounded.
9th	Cpl. McNab	
"	" Colfar	Wounded (at Duty)
"	Pnr. Appleton	
11th	C.S.M. Matthews	
"	Spr. Palmer	Killed.
"	Spr. Harrison	
12th	Spr. Terrell	Wounded (at duty)
14th	L/Cpl. Buck	awarded the MILITARY MEDAL
"	Spr. Plummer	" MILITARY MEDAL
19th	Sgt. Shaw F.	awarded the DISTINGUISHED CONDUCT MEDAL
"	Cpl Townsend	
"	" Colfar	
"	Spr. Watson	awarded the MILITARY MEDAL
"	" Hilding	
June 19th 1917	Lieut J.E. HUCKSTEP R.E. awarded the MILITARY CROSS.

[signature]
Major R.E.
O.C. 101 Fd Coy R.E.

Vol R.E. 24

War Diary

of

101st Field Company.

From

July 1st 1917

July 31st 1917

Volume 23

WAR DIARY
INTELLIGENCE SUMMARY

Army Form C. 2118.

101st Field Company R.E.

JULY

Place	Date	Hour	Summary of Events and Information	Remarks and references to Appendices
DICKEBUSCH	July 1		No 1 Section on fatigues in Camp. Nos 2 & 4 sections on railway repairs and building roads for dump at I31A. No 3 section repairing huts at Reninghelst. Lieut Allen went on leave. Lt Griffin and Lt Huckstep returned from leave.	
	2		Sections continue on same work. A certain amount of shelling in the morning when Nos 2 & 4 sections were working. A Mule (belonging to No 1 Sec) looking with No 1 section was brought back to the Camp badly hit and had to be shot. Sapper BRICKELL.F. (No 4 Section) was badly wounded took no reveal.	
	3		on the works at about 8 AM. Lieut HUCKSTEP proceeded to hospital Dismounted. The King H.M. The King passed by motor in the direction of VIERSTRAAT. The Prince of Wales followed in another car. The Coy lined the road and cheered. First news of Russian Offensive. No work except fatigues.	
	4		Nos 1 & 3 sections with one platoon attached infantry commenced work on trig. stand at MILLE KRUIS Triangle.	
	5		Sections continue on same work. Parties on burying of Coy wagons. O.C. decides to give a prize of 20 francs any month to toolcart men for the best kept tool and forage carts. Hanneries inspected at 2 P.M.	

Army Form C. 2118.

WAR DIARY
or
INTELLIGENCE SUMMARY. J 101 Field Coy. R E

(Erase heading not required.)

JULY

Place	Date	Hour	Summary of Events and Information	Remarks and references to Appendices
	6th		No 1 & 3 sections continue work on Lury siding at MILL KRUIS with one platoon attached to forty (3DLI). No 2 & 4 sections continue sawmill work. Pontoons in VERNOZEPELE dump completed. Lt HUCKSTER and O.C. sighted ammunition dump at N.1 central on MILLE KRUIS - OUDERDOM road. C.R.E. called in the afternoon. One officer and 10 O.R. to proceed to LARCH WOOD tomorrow for work with 128 Fd Coy R.E.	
	7th		A coop few shells from a H.V. Gun fell in this camp at about 4 AM but did no damage. No 1 section continue on Lury siding with one platoon 13th D.L.I and also road repair work near DICKEBUSH LAKE. No 3 section commenced work on ammunition dump at N.1 central with the overseers louries of 6th frames. No 2 & 4 sections continue on light railway work. 11 Lt HAMILTON with 10 OR proceeded to LARCH WOOD camp to work with 128 Coy R.E. Sections digging shelters for platoon in field. Their late Capt Kay returned from leave.	
	8th		Sections continue on their respective works. Motor cycle drawn from 33rd Aux. M.T. Coy 8th. C. A Little wagon horse died at about 6.15 PM after having worked all day, its death was due to collis. 13thDLI/henri 6 coy 10thNF G dump.	
	9th		No 3 section commences T.M. dump else continue work on R.R.P. Other sections other commenced of their platoon 70 Fd Amb Rubber lining Station commenced	

Army Form C. 2118.

101 Field Coy RE

WAR DIARY or INTELLIGENCE SUMMARY

(Erase heading not required.)

JULY 1917

Place	Date	Hour	Summary of Events and Information	Remarks and references to Appendices
to	10th		Works of all sections continue.	
	11th		Company base at rest day. All sections not entire expected for Wot. Church parade at 9AM. A Coy Commissioner after the service, only four officers and the R.S.M. and two men attended the totts. At about 2.30 PM two German aeroplanes came over and destroyed four Observation Balloons by firing at them with incendiary bullets. Great excitement in the camp. The 104th Field Coy arrived in the evening and the 12th N&C + D Sections camp arrived in the afternoon and encamped close to our billets. Enemy aeroplanes also came over in the evening to carry out third honour. Company pays.	
	12th		No 4 Section working with this body. Oliver section on lorry riding. 2nd Lieut ARTUS S.C. the Military Gross.	
	13th		Lt ALLEN relieved from leave. All sections continue on their respective works. OC's orderly S/v Clark got wounded. A few H.V shells dropped near the camp at about 8 PM.	
	14th		Work as usual. Lt Allow relieved Lt HAMILTON in the line at LARCHWOOD	
	15th		Lt HUGKSTEP started to reconnoitre and plot existing trenches. Lt Russell away No 3 section on lorry riding.	

2353 Wt. W2544/1454 700,000 5/15 D. D. & L. A.D.S.S./Forms/C. 2118.

WAR DIARY
or
INTELLIGENCE SUMMARY.

(Erase heading not required.)

Army Form C. 2118.

101st Field Coy RE

JULY 1917

Place	Date	Hour	Summary of Events and Information	Remarks and references to Appendices
	16th		Major TURNER (OC) had an accident on a motor bike and was taken to No 10 C.C.S. in afternoon and returned two hours afterwards. CRE visited Company in the Spoil Bank to Hill 60. The thin to continue from Zillebeke to Davidson Street, he also ordered alterations in the tiroek made by HARTUS.	

Army Form C. 2118.

WAR DIARY
or
INTELLIGENCE SUMMARY.
(Erase heading not required.)

July 1917   101st Field Company R.E.

Place	Date	Hour	Summary of Events and Information	Remarks and references to Appendices
	17th		Captain GRIFFEN and Lt ARTHUS reconnoitred routes for new tracks and deviations to existing ones. Materials for same commenced to go up this evening. Lt HUCHETEE completed reconnaissance of Road Tracks and marked same on map supplied.	
	18th		O. Track completed today	
	19th		Lt. G. SMITH 10th N.F. (attached Coy) killed today and Sapper CLIFF (No 232870) wounded by shell. Sapper GIBSON and L/C GREENWOOD attended Court martial of Divisional Headquarters.	
	20th		B. Batch shelled about 12.15 a.m. no casualties, 3 shell, no damage, slightly crushed by runaway horses. P. Track completed by No 4 Section.	
	21st		Sr Allan and 10 men of No 2 Section returned today from 128th Field Company. The Camp was shelled from 4 P.M. with H.E. and Shrapnel. Shelling continued until about 2 a.m. 22/7/17. 1 man (Foster) wounded, 14 light draught horse mules being hit, also two pontoon wagons damaged beyond repair	
	22nd		Major TURNER returned to Coy in the evening. General BABINGTON inspected medals and certificates tracing in the afternoon.	
	23rd		Camp was moved about a quarter of a mile south of old position owing to the night shelling. Previous commenced formation level of brigade road running from Chester Farm to Knoll Road.	

WAR DIARY or INTELLIGENCE SUMMARY

Army Form C. 2118.

101st Fd Coy RE

JULY

Place	Date	Hour	Summary of Events and Information	Remarks and references to Appendices
	24		Nos 2 & 4 Sections commenced work on Shelfwood. Starting at L.R. head to its rear BLAUVE PORT and covering trench. CHESTER FARM, While on the job 2 men were killed and 5 men injured owing to enemy shell fire caused by explosion. Cooper & Crockett were the lives suffering who were killed.	
	25		No 1 & 3 Sections continued work and completed 80 yards of fighting trench. and Spr CROCKETT was buried.	
	26		No 2 & 4 Sections continued on road. No 3 & 4 along tube pipes in camp fell at 12.30 PM. The Company had a civilian unable to remain. The 133 A.T. Coy RE and 4 men lay about to move.	
	27		No 1 & 3 Sections on Shelfwood. No 2 & 4 on Cawl tube pipes diverting shell. Relieved by No. 11 Coy Shr Hancock died of injuries receiving from shell, Spr Grison, Suwark, Smith and Todd. Sprs Ribson in sk enlisted to live.	
	28			
	29		No 1 & 3 Sections on road. N/Cpl Gillespie was hit in the lung and taken to the dressing station. He received very bad in the evening.	
	30		No 2 & 4 Sections on road. Sorry to say 21 Cpl Gillespie died on the 29th. Instructions from C.R. II Corps that we work to the clear on road tomorrow.	

Army Form C. 2118.

WAR DIARY
or
~~INTELLIGENCE SUMMARY~~

101st Field Coy. RE

(Erase heading not required.)

JULY

Place	Date	Hour	Summary of Events and Information	Remarks and references to Appendices
	31		British Offensive commenced at 4 A.M. after several days bombardment. Several hundred prisoners passed by our camp. Company did not work. Company beat G.S. Staff (Romero) at cricket in the afternoon.	Railway RE

Vol 25
R.E

War Diary

101st Field Company.

From

August 1st 1914

to

August 31st 1914.

Volume 24.

AUGUST 1917

101st Field Coy RE   Army Form C. 2118.

WAR DIARY
or
INTELLIGENCE SUMMARY.
(Erase heading not required.)

Army Form C. 2118.

Place	Date	Hour	Summary of Events and Information	Remarks and references to Appendices
	1		Very heavy rain all day. No work done on road. Camp was very nearly flooded out but saved by officers and men clearing out and digging drains. Two pontoon bridges received in pieces & those that were destroyed by shell fire.	
	2		Nos 1+3 sections went out but finished in about two hours owing to heavy rain. Rained hard all day but men to repair to work on drains. The smoke line has been kept clear. Received hand of day.	
	3		No work on road owing to state of weather. Received hand of day.	
	4		Nos 4 between 2 & 4 section worked on road and completed up to the VERBRANDEN MOLEN ROAD — Very heavy showers of rain during the day.	
	5		No work. C.R.E. called at about 11.30 AM. Several reinforcements arrived.	
	6		Nos 1 + 3 sections worked on road — Repairs completed. The work is now beyond VERBRANDEN ROAD.	
	7		No work. Nos 2 & 4 sections on fatigues. Company fils arms to were issued to & be attached to 184 Coys.	
	8		Company moved (It. off 9 AM and for & this division (about ½ a mile in front of YLAMERTINGHE on N. side of VLAMERTINGHE - YPRES road) at 10 AM. Transport arrived at 1 PM and after unloading returning to Coy's lines to load a train at G.S.b. 09 about 2 miles East of POPERINGHE. Two fatigues were counted in the evening owing to enemy shelling the road by the camp.	A.S.Duff

2353 Wt. W2544/1454 700,000 5/15 D. D. & L.   A.D.S.S./Forms/C. 2118.

WAR DIARY or INTELLIGENCE SUMMARY

Army Form C. 2118.

101 Fld Coy
R.E.

AUGUST

Place	Date	Hour	Summary of Events and Information	Remarks and references to Appendices
	9		The O.C. found that Coy were too far away so we moved back to the horse lines and built a camp to hold the whole company. Taken on camp construction the whole day. 2/Lt HAMILTON joined this Coy.	
	10	8 A.M.	Parade. Sections drilling for one hour after which they finished building the camp. O.C. (Maj TURNER) went on leave. 2/Lt HAMILTON joined to Coy and went on leave.	
	11	8 A.M.	Parade. Fatigues.	
	12	9 A.M.	No work. Driver ATKINSON R.E. injured whilst exercising	
	13		Inter section football matches in afternoon. Irish Engineers knocked out Coopie. Drivers beat No. 1 K.O. No. 4 beat No. 3 in 2.	
	14		2 Pack animals came to company. Drivers drew uhy No 2 in K.O. No. 4 beat we in leape. 2/Lt D horse joined company.	
	15		Fatigues	
	16		No 1+2 sections NCO's doing war references. Football co-operating in the afternoon. "	
	17		No 3+4 sections NCO's doing "	
	18		Aeroplane Coy had half an hours Gas practise from 9.30 P.M. to 10 P.M.	
	19		During the practise a German aeroplane dropped two bombs very near the camp	
(20)				

Army Form C. 2118.

WAR DIARY
or
INTELLIGENCE SUMMARY.

101st Field Coy. R.E.

August

(Erase heading not required.)

Place	Date	Hour	Summary of Events and Information	Remarks and references to Appendices
	19		Fired in toretion cup walls. No 4 sectn bent N.O.R. by 28. 6.1	
	20		Company moved to H.Q.2.C. Coy forward billets about a mile in front of VLAMERTINGHE. No 4 sectn commenced work on ADMIRAL'S ROAD tomorrow. H.Q.&C. Coy to remain in same place.	
	21		No 1&2&3 sections with this pltoon started work on ADMIRAL'S road. 6.30 A.M. at about 9.30 A.M. the German commenced a heavy bombardment. It lasted by several shrapnels and a few H.E. shells bursting on and around (between) and very soon a hell of every calibre was falling in the neighbourhood. BUFF'S ROAD ADMIRALS ROAD and BOUNDARY ROAD was & hells and also all the tropelan area between their meals. At about 4.45 A.M. the shelling became very much less in time and their went round to try and collect men and tools. The casualties was as follows. Spr EDWARDS and Spr COLLEY killed. Lt HUCKSTEP slightly wounded and 9 O.R. wounded and seven of which were evacuated.	
	22.		No 13th section on work. They were trialed by Gas for the first hour or so but after that they had a comparatively quiet day. Lt HAMILTON Returned from leave.	

2353 Wt. W2544/1454 700,000 5/15 D. D. & L. A.D.S.S./Forms/C. 2118.

WAR DIARY or INTELLIGENCE SUMMARY

August 101st Field Coy. R.E.

Army Form C. 2118.

Place	Date	Hour	Summary of Events and Information	Remarks and references to Appendices
	23.		No 1 & 4 Sections worked on road. Except for a little shelling in the early morning they had a quiet day. OC returned from leave.	
	24		No 2 & 4 sections working. Reproduction from 374 R. Coy came to work our camp.	
	25		Lt HAMILTON and INTERPRETER Company boy went to inspect new billets near OUDERDOM in DEVONSHIRE CAMP area. Orders came in later not to remove to this camp. Lieut ALLEN went to take over forward billets and not DEVONSHIRE CAMP. Sappers sent down to take over camp from 61st Fd Coy R.E. 50 of 4th Fd Coy given both our camp in evening.	
	2̶5̶ 26.		Company moved at 6 AM. Stopped at CAFÉ BELGE on the DICKIE BUSH KRUISTRAAT Road. No 2 & 4 Sections went up to Railway dugouts. No 1 Section stayed at Cafe Belge camp. H.Q.ers went to line behind DICKIE BUSH. The accommodation at Café Belge camp is very bad. It rained the whole night and everybody got wet and practically flooded out. OC went to see CRE to find out about works	
	27		The Company have been doing the following works to carry out later Two coming offensive. 2 Tracks to make, one from ZILLEBEKE to STIRLING CASTLE, one from ZILLEBEKE to CLAPHAM Junction. Two water storage points. One new Stirling Castle, one Clapham Junction. Gas visual signalling station from Clapham junction. Stores to be put up at Clapham junction & Krinks to work the Stirling points. Two dealers at RAILWAY DUGOUTS are busy all day are being entries accommodation for the work of the Eng. and others.	

WAR DIARY or INTELLIGENCE SUMMARY

Army Form C. 2118.

Place	Date	Hour	Summary of Events and Information	Remarks and references to Appendices
RAILWAY DUGOUTS YPRES.	28		Section 2 & 4 continued on works and roads (west) proper. Particularly the shelling estab. in the morning. 12 Thurles wood this journey to old German front line this from ZIMF to K1, carrying petards etc. Beyond the old German front line the ground is in a very bad state and consists of one huge area of intensely shell holes. It rained very hard all day.	
	29		The white Coy in now established at Railway dugouts. No 1 & 3 worked today. Mules continued to carry stores, trades & large parties completed also VISUAL Signalling station. A good deal of rain during the day.	
	30		No 2 & 4 sections or works. Mules carrying stores to SANCTUARY WOOD dump. Lt ROSSELL went on leave.	
	31		No 1 & 3 on works. A good deal of shelling w/r no casualties. In the afternoon several German aeroplanes came over and bombed (no hurts came on the town) feld in the town lines, C.Q.M.S. Nightingale also wounded during delivery and also killed. Mort of 4 to R.S.E. This is vertu RE road about very badly and drive [illegible] 15 in houses. 2 casualties in man and 15 in horses.	

C.R. Griffin
for O.C. 177 McKenzie?

Vol 26

War Diary
101st Field Company. R.E.

from
1st September 1917
to
30th September 1917.

Volume 25

Army Form C. 2118.

SEPTEMBER
WAR DIARY
or
~~AUGUST~~ INTELLIGENCE SUMMARY.   105th Field Coy. RE

Instructions regarding War Diaries and Intelligence Summaries are contained in F. S. Regs., Part II. and the Staff Manual respectively. Title pages will be prepared in manuscript.

Place	Date	Hour	Summary of Events and Information	Remarks and references to Appendices
RAILWAY DUGOUTS	1		No 2 & 4 Sections on work. C.Q.M.S. NIGHTINGALE was buried was DICKIE BUSH. Driver KELSEY died of wounds.	
	2		No 1 & 3 Sections on work.	
	3		A German aeroplane put a bomb right in the middle of our horse lines causing the death of twenty nine and wounding twenty one so severely that they had to be destroyed. This is nearly 75% of our horses. No 1 & 3 sections were sent for in the afternoon from Railway Dugouts. They had to dig a grave large enough to bury the horses in. It was 3 P.M. when they started work and 9 P.M. when they finished. between detachments remounts were obtained from the 5th Army Remount Station. We have orders for early tomorrow morning	
BERTHEN	4		The Coy moved to the BERTHEN area. the horses & transport left. The Hoots pontoons & details all except one had blown up, behind as there were not sufficient lorries. Coy arrived at rest billet (FONTAINE HOUCK) at about 15 hours.	
	5		No work. Twenty two more wounded were evacuated from 3rd Army Remount. The shell of their movement is found one for that they went on practice of moving.	

WAR DIARY

INTELLIGENCE SUMMARY. 10th - 27th W Coy RE

SEPTEMBER

Army Form C. 2118.

Place	Date	Hour	Summary of Events and Information	Remarks and references to Appendices
Berguin	6		Sections doing light training and steady drill in the morning. The Coy had a match (cricket) afternoon won by two runs. The two Pontoons which were left at DICKIEBUSH were sent for.	
	7		Sections doing light training in the morning.	
	8		Divisional Football Cup Final G&Forts Staff at Company Day. Divisional Football Cup had their sports and cricket. S. Staff beaten. J.S. Staff had this sports and in third all round.	
	9		Church parade in the morning. 9 Soh Staff (Pioneers) play the Divisional field Coys at cricket — Field Coys win. Major Turner celebrated the end of his third year in France.	
	10		Sections training in the morning and preparing course for wounded sports.	
	11		The Coy and the 128 Coy had a combined wounded sports.	
	12		Lieut. RUSSELL returned from leave. Parties for billing and lathes ever took in the line.	

Army Form C. 2118.

WAR DIARY or INTELLIGENCE SUMMARY.

SEPTEMBER — 101st Field Coy. R.E.

Date	Hour	Summary of Events and Information	Remarks and references to Appendices
13		Company moved to ONTARIO Camp near RENINGHELST.	
14		Company moved to DICKEBUSH (South of church). Nos 2 & 4 sections to straight to Railway Dugouts.	
15		Nos 2 & 4 sections working up this line — Nos 1 & 3 doing back area work attached infantry as follows. 8th Yorks 9th Yorks Duke of Wellingtons and West Riding each supply 25 men & Infantry officers 11/15 Robinson 8th Yorks at Woodcote Ho.	
16		Work as usual on tracks and dugouts.	
17		Work on tracks and at Bedford House.	
18		Nos 2 & 4 sections relieved from Railway Dugouts.	
19		Company rest.	
20		2nd and 5th Armies attack on an eight mile front from between LANGEMARCK and KLEIN ZILLEBEKE. No 1 Sect: under Lieut RUSSELL and No 3 under Lt HUCKSTEP made shoft tracks on this field between INVERNESS COPSE and VELDHOEK, if the MENIN ROAD. Total casualties in R.E. section have been one wounded.	

SEPTEMBER WAR DIARY or INTELLIGENCE SUMMARY

101st Fd. Coy. RE

Army Form C. 2118.

Place	Date	Hour	Summary of Events and Information	Remarks and references to Appendices
	21		No 2 & 4 sections commenced a communication trench from J AP AVENUE to NORTHAMPTON FARM. They would have finished only the Q.S. Staff Pioneers (who were to help them) turned up. This was done at night.	
	22		No 1 & 2 sections completed communication trench.	
	23		Petrouille time from 11th Fd Eng. took over work. Lt Allen went to BOESCHEPE billets. Coy moved to BOESCHÈPE.	
No BOESCHÈPE	24		Coy commenced work on x"cape dehorts, working under C.RE	
	25		x"cape po.	
	26		All sections working. At about 10PM a German aeroplane	
	27		All sections working. dropped a bomb about 50 yards from the hora lines. There were no casualties.	
	28		Sections work in the morning only.	
	29		Drivers and seven NCO's were paid.	
	30		Lt Antus went on leave. No work. Voluntary church service 11AM.	

Griffith Cubbert F Major
Fr 101 Fd Coy RE

CONFIDENTIAL

WAR DIARY

OF

101st FIELD COMPANY. R.E.

FROM

OCTOBER 1st 1917.

TO

OCTOBER 31st 1917.

VOLUME 26.

WAR DIARY

OCTOBER 1917   101st Field Coy R.E.

INTELLIGENCE SUMMARY

Army Form C. 2118.

Place	Date	Hour	Summary of Events and Information	Remarks and references to Appendices
BOESCHEPE	1		Company work as usual	
"	2		" " " "	
"	3		" " " "	
"	4		Horses moved to good standings in the artillery camp. A good many showers during the day	
"	5		Went to boat weather. The OC went tomorrow for the sappers to work with. Nissen huts built for the 2 schools. The weather has commenced to get very cold.	
"	6		The school was the town Officers mess this were town Officers. Orders to put clothes on in the artillery camp. Lights out hour at 12 midnight.	
"	7		Company work. Parades 9AM and 2 PM. At about 10 PM the Artillery Camp was also fire. We had three horses out of which two perished. Sappers up in arms to DAC which have just come in. Sappers are still busy at the school - horses are back at the old place and were also.	
"	8		Work as usual. Iubilantis GORTHALS leaves the company and Pay No. 1 & 44 rations. Iubilantis SLOTHU at METERIN and Laundry firms or Camping division near VIATOU.	
"	9		at BESACE Farm taken in hand.	

Arthur Capel R.E.

WAR DIARY or INTELLIGENCE SUMMARY

Army Form C. 2118.

OCTOBER 1917

101st Field Coy RE

Place	Date	Hour	Summary of Events and Information	Remarks and references to Appendices
Nr BOESCHEPE	10		2/Cpl O'Dowell & 2/Cpl Whitehouse & Cpl Davies received Military Medals on September 20th in Battle of Menin Road. Coy gets orders to move with Division – the an to be the near Company. Lt HAMILTON and 6 cyclists sent to report to RE Dump & carry on work until relief. Lt RUSS & Lt/k Company.	
Chateau Segard	11		Coy moved to near Chateau Segard about 2 mile east of DICKEBUSCH. Billeted in old dugouts in the strong point around the remains of the Chateau.	
"	12		No 2 Section goes up to maintain plank road north of HOOGE. Lt HAMILTON returned to Company.	
13			Lt HAILTON works on road. No 3 Sect: works on @ the slab.	
	14		Lt Astos returned from leave. Works on Div HQ 11000R and later to BOYDESVELDE. Lt Anlin wounded near 11000R and later taken to BOYDESVELDE. Such driving rain commenced at Zillebeke BOND. Party in barn billets. Horse standing covered in prepan.	
	15		Work as usual.	
	16		Work as usual.	
	17		Lt CRASWELLER joined Company and was posted to No 4 Section.	
	18		Work as usual.	

Arthur Cooper

WAR DIARY
or
~~INTELLIGENCE~~ SUMMARY

Army Form C. 2118.

OCTOBER   101st Field Coy R.E.

Place	Date	Hour	Summary of Events and Information	Remarks and references to Appendices
Chateau SEGARD	19		No1 section commenced beking near ZILLEBEKE BOND. Drivers CHEEVERS & BILTON were badly wounded at SHARPNEL CORNER while coming back from the Bend. The train of four mules was killed. In the afternoon at about 3PM "Lt A.D. HAMILTON was killed while on the job at ZILLEBEKE BOND also Spr HOBBS and POWELL were wounded at the same time. "Lt BLEWIT joined the company and took over No3 sect from Lt HUCKSTEP M.E.	
	20		"Lt HAMILTON was buried at 10AM at LACLYTTE Cemetery. "Lt WILSON joined company and took over No1 Section.	
	21		Lt HUCKSTEP M.E. left the Coy to join the 162 Fd Coy to act as second in command. Coy with new work from 126 Fd Coy RE working under CRE X Corps.	
	22.		Coy commenced work for CRE X Corps.	
	23.		Lieut WALLER rejoined company from 23rd Div Wing Company. Worked on putting C.R.E. X Corps.	
	24.		Company work as usual.	
	25.		" " " "	
	26.		" " " "	
	27		" " " " 2nd Lieut W.A. KIRK joining Company. Capt GRIFFIN went on leave.	

Army Form C. 2118.

OCTOBER

WAR DIARY
or
INTELLIGENCE SUMMARY.

(Erase heading not required.)

Instructions regarding War Diaries and Intelligence Summaries are contained in F. S. Regs., Part II. and the Staff Manual respectively. Title pages will be prepared in manuscript.

Place	Date	Hour	Summary of Events and Information	Remarks and references to Appendices
CHATEAU SEGARD	28.		Came to any worked during morning. Got under orders at 12 (noon). Company marched to BOESCHEPE and camped at 6.10 p.m.	
BOESCHEPE	29.		Company rested. Capt GRIFFIN recalled from leave.	
	30.		—	
	31.		Sections drilled in morning. Capt GRIFFIN returned from leave.	

Ashton Capt
for O/C Coy
31.10.15

www.ingramcontent.com/pod-product-compliance
Lightning Source LLC
Chambersburg PA
CBHW081548160426
43191CB00011B/1868